Marching Toward Freedom

MARCHING TOWARD FREEDOM

1957-1965

FROM THE FOUNDING
OF THE SOUTHERN CHRISTIAN
LEADERSHIP CONFERENCE
TO THE ASSASSINATION
OF MALCOLM X

Robert Weisbrot

CHELSEA HOUSE PUBLISHERS
New York   Philadelphia

FRONTISPIECE   Forgetting their wide philosophical differences, the Reverend Martin Luther King, Jr., and Black Muslim leader Malcolm X exchange handshakes and smiles in Washington, D.C., in 1964.

ON THE COVER   The Reverend Martin Luther King, Jr. (center front), meets with other civil rights leaders in the late 1950s. Standing second from the left is the Reverend Ralph D. Abernathy; the Reverend Fred L. Shuttlesworth is seated at King's left shoulder.

Chelsea House Publishers
Editorial Director   Richard Rennert
Executive Managing Editor   Karyn Gullen Browne
Copy Chief   Robin James
Picture Editor   Adrian G. Allen
Art Director   Robert Mitchell
Manufacturing Director   Gerald Levine

Milestones in Black American History
Senior Editor   Marian W. Taylor
Series Originator and Adviser   Benjamin I. Cohen
Series Consultants   Clayborne Carson, Darlene Clark Hine
Series Designer   Rae Grant

Staff for MARCHING TOWARD FREEDOM
Editorial Assistant   Annie McDonnell
Picture Researcher   Alan Gottlieb

First Printing

1 3 5 7 9 8 6 4 2

Library of Congress Cataloging-in-Publication Data

Weisbrot, Robert.
    Marching toward freedom, 1957–1965 : from the founding of the Southern Christian Leadership Conference to the assassination of Malcolm X / Robert Weisbrot.
        p. cm.—(Milestones in Black American history)
    Includes bibliographical references (p.).
        ISBN 0-7910-2256-0.
        ISBN 0-7910-2682-5 (pbk.)
    1. Afro-Americans—Civil rights. 2. Civil rights movements—United States—History—20th century. 3. Southern States—Race relations. 4. Afro-Americans—History—1877–1964. I. Series.
E185.61.W395 1994   93-11964
973'.0496073—dc20   CIP
                                                                              Rev

CONTENTS

18.95

MILESTONES IN BLACK AMERICAN HISTORY

INTRODUCTION

The years between 1957 and 1965 marked a revolution in the black American experience; in few periods of U.S. history has a people's destiny changed more sharply or more swiftly.

Although the Supreme Court had outlawed public school segregation in 1954, only one percent of southern black children attended integrated schools in 1957. That year, when nine black students tried to enter Central High School in Little Rock, Arkansas, federal troops had to protect them from surging white mobs. Across the South, the Ku Klux Klan and other white-supremacist groups continued to keep well over half of the black population away from the polls. In 1957, segregation still ruled the land, not just in schools but in trains, restaurants, parks, public rest rooms, beaches, building entrances, movie theaters—and even in cemeteries.

The revolution brought to the fore a new generation of southern black activists, including an eloquent young black clergyman named Martin Luther King, Jr. Early in 1957, fresh from a triumphant protest against bus segregation in Montgomery, Alabama, King formed the Southern Christian Leadership Conference (SCLC), a group of some 60 black civil rights leaders seeking ways to expand the nonviolent campaigns for racial equality.

The black revolution surged ahead so rapidly that its leaders often had to hurry after ordinary citizens who were starting their own protests against segregation. In February 1960, four teenage black college students defied southern law and seated themselves at a whites-only lunch counter in North Carolina. This act of courage inspired many similar demands for civil rights from Maryland to Mississippi. During the next five years, a host of Americans dedicated—and

Surrounded by cheering supporters and backed by his wife, Coretta, the Reverend Martin Luther King, Jr.(in dark suit,center), beams after his 1956 conviction for conspiring to boycott segregated buses in Montgomery, Alabama. King's trial received widespread news coverage and gave fresh momentum to the young civil rights movement.

sometimes lost—their lives to wresting social justice from a stubborn, segregationist society. For civil rights marchers in these tumultuous years, the road did not run straight, nor did it always run upward. But they marched on.

These were the years of SCLC, NAACP, SNCC, CORE; the years of sit-ins, swim-ins, pray-ins; of beatings and mass arrests; of marches, boycotts, and Freedom Rides; of snarling police dogs and magnum-force fire hoses; of flamboyant oratory and quiet courage; of a million voices singing "We Shall Overcome." They were the years, too, of confrontation: Governor George Wallace of Alabama, pledging "Segregation forever!" defended white supremacy alongside such allies as

Mississippi's governor Ross Barnett, Arkansas governor Orval Faubus, and Alabama sheriffs Bull Connor and Big Jim Clark. Representing the new order was a legion of civil rights warriors, including King, James Farmer, A. Philip Randolph, the Reverend Fred Shuttlesworth, Bayard Rustin, Bob Moses, and Medgar Evers, along with militant Black Muslims Elijah Muhammad and Malcolm X. The Muslims' breakaway young firebrand, Malcolm attracted thousands of followers before falling to assassins' bullets in 1965. These crowded years also encompassed the greatest protest demonstration in American history. "I have a dream," said Martin Luther King, Jr., at the 1963 March on Washington.

Finally, in 1964, the U.S. Congress passed a civil rights bill aimed at enabling blacks to compete for America's prizes. White and Colored signs suddenly came down, and the government struck hard at the Klan and other hate groups. By the end of the decade southern schools had begun to teach black and white pupils together. The Voting Rights Act of 1965 led to a vast increase in southern black registration and to the election of thousands of black officials—including more than one Alabama sheriff. Now there was no turning back. Racism and poverty continued to challenge black America, but in the space of only eight years, the nation had entered a new era. From this point on, "We the people of the United States" would mean *all* the people of the United States.

MILESTONES
1957-65

1957

January: SCLC Begins

- The Reverend Martin Luther King, Jr., establishes the Southern Christian Leadership Conference (SCLC) in Atlanta, Georgia. Joining King in the new organization are 60 black leaders who later form a network of local groups devoted to applying "nonviolent direct action" against Jim Crow (racial discrimination).

May: Civil Rights Bill

- The SCLC, backed by the National Association for the Advancement of Colored People (NAACP), stages a Washington rally, or "Prayer Pilgrimage," to urge congressional passage of a black voting-rights bill. The event draws some 25,000 people, and the bill—a mild measure, but the first in nearly a century aimed at the protection of black civil rights—is passed.

September: Showdown in Arkansas

- A federal court orders segregated public schools in Little Rock to start accepting blacks. Arkansas governor Orval Faubus responds by sending the National Guard to keep blacks out of the schools. After threats of mob violence, President Dwight Eisenhower sends troops to enforce the court order, and nine black students finally enroll in Little Rock's Central High School.

1959

March: Black Lights on Broadway

- Playwright Lorraine Hansberry's *A Raisin in the Sun* opens in New York City. Starring Claudia McNeil, Ruby Dee, and Sidney Poitier, the drama about black ghetto life will enjoy the longest run up to that time of any play by a black author. *Raisin* is directed by Lloyd Richards, Broadway's first black director in more than 50 years.

1960

February: Birth of the Sit-in

- Four black students from North Carolina Agricultural and Technical College in Greensboro, North Carolina, take seats at a Woolworth's "whites-only" lunch counter. The daring move inspires a nationwide wave of integrationist "sit-ins," "pray-ins," and "swim-ins."

March: Georgians Enter the Battle

- Atlanta University student Julian Bond and a dozen colleagues try to buy a meal at the municipal cafeteria in City Hall. The young people are arrested and jailed. Five years later, the 25-year-old Bond wins election to the Georgia House of Representatives.

April: The Start of Snick

- Students at Shaw University in Raleigh, North Carolina, establish the Student Nonviolent Coordinating Committee (SNCC, pronounced "Snick").

July: Sit-in Victory; Words from the Nation

- The Woolworth's lunch counter in Greensboro, North Carolina, starts serving black as well as white customers.
- Elijah Muhammad, leader of the nationalist-religious movement known as the Nation of Islam, or the Black Muslims, calls for the establishment of an all-black state. The Nation announces a membership of 100,000, a number attributed largely to the work of the dynamic young minister Malcolm X.

September: Black Gold

- Cassius Clay, an 18-year-old light heavyweight boxer from Kentucky, wins an Olympic gold medal in Rome, Italy. Back in his native state, Clay—later known as world heavyweight champion Muhammad Ali—is refused service in a restaurant because of his race. He tosses his medal into the Ohio River.

1961

February: Black Men in High Places

- President Kennedy appoints Harvard-educated housing expert Robert Weaver administrator of the Housing and Home Finance Agency. It is the highest federal post yet held by an African American.
- Subsequent Kennedy appointments include that of James B. Parsons to the District Court of Northern Illinois, a move that makes Parsons the first black federal judge in the continental United States. Kennedy next appoints Thurgood Marshall, chief counsel of the NAACP, to the position of associate judge on the Second Circuit Court of Appeals.
- Among the year's other black political achievements are the election of lawyer Edward W. Brooke to the post of Massachusetts attorney general, which makes him New England's highest ranking black official; the election to the Georgia State Senate of Leroy Johnson, the first black to so serve since Reconstruction; and the election of California's first black U.S. congressman, Augustus Hawkins.

May: Destination—Liberty

- Freedom Riders, an interracial band of mostly young people led by James Farmer of the Congress of Racial Equality (CORE), begin a swing through the South by bus. The riders hope to expose—and thereby end—segregation in bus terminals. Riders are harassed, beaten, and jailed; one of their buses is seized and burned by white hooligans near Anniston, Alabama. But they continue. In September, the Interstate Commerce Commission rules that segregation in interstate travel facilities is illegal.

August: Entering Mississippi

- Robert Moses and other SNCC volunteers begin the Voter Education Project in McComb, Mississippi. The effort, which will continue for four years and eventually involve both white and black volunteers, will revolutionize voting patterns in the Deep South.

1962

September: "Ole Miss" Caves In

- James Meredith becomes the first black student at the University of Mississippi. His admission follows violent rioting, which is ended only by the intercession of state troopers, National Guardsmen, and federal marshals.

1963

April: Victory in Birmingham

- The SCLC launches a series of antisegregation demonstrations in Birmingham, Alabama. As the protests continue, Police Chief "Bull" Connor and his men attack participants with water cannons, police dogs, truncheons, and mass arrests. Among those jailed is Martin Luther King, Jr., who writes his celebrated "Letter from Birmingham Jail" at this time. After a month of much-publicized violence, Birmingham officials agree to a desegregation plan, hailed by the SCLC's Fred Shuttlesworth as a victory for "human supremacy."

June: Wallace at the Gate

- Pledging to preserve "Segregation forever!" Governor George Wallace of Alabama stands at the University of Alabama's doors to prevent entry of two black students. Under orders from the U.S. attorney general, the university backs down and the students enroll. President John F. Kennedy hails the students' triumph, asserts that "race has no place in American life or law," and asks Congress for a sweeping new civil rights measure.
- Medgar Evers, head of the Mississippi NAACP, is ambushed and murdered near his home in Jackson, Mississippi.

August: Du Bois and King

- William Edward Burghardt Du Bois, an NAACP founder and longtime editor of its publication *The Crisis*, author, and educator, dies in Ghana, Africa, at the age of 95.
- More than 250,000 people assemble in the nation's capital to participate in a March on Washington, to this date the largest protest demonstration in American history. Speaking out for civil rights at the march are both whites and blacks, including America's most prominent black leaders. Martin Luther King, Jr., electrifies the crowd with an impassioned speech beginning, "I have a dream."

September: Death in Alabama

- A blast rocks a black Baptist church, killing four girls in a Sunday school class. No arrests are made, and no riots break out.

November: Death in Texas

- President John F. Kennedy is assassinated in Dallas, Texas; at his death, Congress is still debating his civil rights proposals.

December: Black Medalists

- Kennedy's successor, Lyndon Johnson, awards the nation's highest civilian decoration, the Medal of Freedom, to legendary contralto Marian Anderson and international diplomat and human rights crusader Ralph J. Bunche.

1964

January: Washington Arrival; New Amendment

- President Johnson appoints journalist Carl T. Rowan director of the United States Information Agency, a body never before run by an African American.
- The nation ratifies the Constitution's Twenty-fourth Amendment, which eliminates the use of the poll tax—historically used to keep blacks from voting—in presidential elections.

April: Hollywood Highlight

- Sidney Poitier becomes the first African American in cinema history to win the Academy Award for Best Actor, earned for his role in *Lilies of the Field*.

July: Civil Rights on the March

- Congress passes the Kennedy-Johnson civil rights bill, the most sweeping rights-reform law since 1875. The measure prohibits discrimination in public accommodations and in employment.

August: Murder in Mississippi

- Three young civil rights workers, James E. Chaney, Michael Schwerner, and Andrew Goodman, are found dead near Philadelphia, Mississippi. The FBI accuses a number of white segregationists, including several law enforcement officers, of the murders.

December: International Glory

- The Reverend Martin Luther King, Jr., receives the Nobel Peace Prize, which he accepts in Oslo, Norway. King, at age 35, is the youngest person and the second African American to receive the much-coveted award.

1965

January: Selma, Alabama; Darkness on Stage

- King leads a voter-registration drive in Selma; white resistance stiffens.
- Playwright Lorraine Hansberry dies of cancer at the age of 34.

February: Murder in Manhattan

- Malcolm X is assassinated in New York City. (A year later, three Black Muslims are convicted of the murder.)

March: "Bloody Sunday"

- Six hundred civil rights activists attempt to march from Selma to Montgomery, Alabama. They are intercepted and attacked by mounted police at Selma's Edmund Pettus Bridge. Ten days later, on March 17, after a federal judge rules the march legal, it begins again, ending successfully with 25,000 people entering Montgomery on March 25.

July: A New Post for Marshall

- Appeals Court judge Thurgood Marshall becomes solicitor general of the United States. He is now the highest-ranking black law-enforcement official in the nation's history.

August: A Nightmare in Watts and a New Rights Law

- Riots break out in the 98-percent-black Watts district of Los Angeles. The racial disturbance—the worst in America to this time—leaves 34 dead, 900 injured, and 4,000 in jail, and inflicts property losses of some $45 million.
- President Johnson signs the landmark Voting Rights Bill, which strikes down all the devices—literacy tests, local rule over voter registration, election taxes, etc.—traditionally used to keep southern blacks from the polls.

September: The Last Paige

- Leroy "Satchel" Paige, the legendary Negro Leagues star who in 1948 became the first black to pitch in the major leagues, makes his final big-league appearance.

Marching Toward Freedom

1

GREENSBORO

FOUR American students started a revolution in early 1960. Perhaps few Americans of the time would have imagined that a quartet of first-year students at North Carolina Agricultural and Technical College (A & T), a black school in Greensboro, were capable of changing America, but history proved they were.

These 18-year-olds had attracted little attention when they joined 3,000 other A & T undergraduates in the fall of 1959. Nor did they seem, on the surface, to have a great deal in common. Ezell Blair, Jr., short and lively, roomed with studious physics major Joseph McNeil; down the hall lived towering, plain-spoken Francis McCain; David Richmond, a slender, shy student who was pondering a future in the ministry, lived in Greensboro. Yet these four teenagers quickly became close friends and helped each other act more boldly than any of them alone might have dreamed possible.

Sit-in founders Joseph McNeil (left) and Francis McCain (second from left) reenact their historic 1960 demonstration at a lunch counter in Greensboro, North Carolina. Joining the pioneers are Clarence Henderson (far right) and Billy Smith, early recruits who helped turn the quiet Greensboro protest into a nationwide action.

17

In the beginning of the school year, the young men's dormitory conversations bounced from great issues of philosophy to the horrors of campus food to the relative charms of the local women. But always their remarks returned to a single, gnawing question: when would blacks do something about the racial barriers that blocked their hopes and mocked their pride?

The students' impatience centered on the failure of the federal government to end the South's "Jim Crow" practices, which separated blacks from whites and treated them as an inferior race. (*Jim Crow* first surfaced in the popular minstrel shows of the 19th century. Wearing black makeup, white comic actors would dance crazily to the refrain, "Jump, Jim Crow!" The term was soon used to describe the antiblack laws of the post–Civil War South; whites also used it as an insulting label for blacks themselves.)

In 1957 Congress had outlawed interference with voting rights because of race, yet blacks who tried to register in much of the South risked their jobs or even their lives. By 1960 blacks had made notable gains in the armed forces, where they were serving in integrated units. At home, however, the legal segregation of many public places reminded returning black veterans that, out of uniform, they ranked no higher than Citizen, Second Class. And in 1960, a full six years after the Supreme Court had ordered an end to segregated education, more than 99 percent of southern black children still attended separate schools.

Night after night, the four A & T students talked on, and their self-questioning became increasingly personal: at what point would they, the younger generation of black Americans, take their stand against injustice? At last, their deepening friendship gave them, in McCain's words, "that little bit of incentive and that little bit of courage." Their discontent with American race relations turned into a specific plan for defiance.

McNeil, Blair, McCain, and Richmond decided to break the South's long tradition of racially segregated dining by sitting at a "whites-only" lunch counter. Their choice of site was the 66-seat, L-shaped counter at F. W. Woolworth, Greensboro's busy five-and-dime store. The single largest money-maker in downtown Greensboro, the Woolworth's lunch counter was also the only spot in the store where blacks were not allowed to make purchases. That counter stood as a symbol of Jim Crow at its most insulting.

As they planned their protest, none of the four students had a clear idea what it would involve. "We'll stay until we get served," said one. Ezell Blair replied, "Well, you know, that might be weeks, that might be months, that might be never." The young men also worried about possible punishment by white authorities and black college officials. But one evening, Francis McCain overcame all doubts. Pounding a dresser, he dared his friends: "Are you guys chicken or not?" The next morning, February 1, 1960, the four friends set out to give Jim Crow a blow he would not forget.

To prove themselves legitimate, paying customers, the students made purchases in different departments of the Woolworth's store. Then came the test at the lunch counter: "Coffee, please." The white waitress replied, "Sorry, we don't serve colored here." But the youths politely persisted. Behind the counter a black dishwasher, who feared for her job and for the young men, gruffly tried to set them straight. "You're acting stupid, ignorant!" she said. They should know, she insisted, that the counter was for white people. "That why we can't get any place today," she added hotly, "because of people like you, rabble-rousers, trouble-makers." To the students, this advice belonged to an age of racial segregation that had already lasted far too long. They listened to the woman patiently, but they did not leave the counter.

A white police officer paced the aisle behind the students, tapping his club against his palm and looking, McCain later recalled, "mean and red and a little bit upset and a little bit disgusted." The four friends were trembling inside. But the officer made no arrests. The students had turned his world upside down, ignoring his presence but acting too quietly and courteously to justify his use of club or gun.

The store manager, too, seemed able to think of no better solution than to let the students sit undisturbed while he acted as though they were not violating his exclusively white lunch counter. Gradually it dawned on the young protesters that, at least for the moment, they had faced down the city's white establishment. "By then," McCain remembered, "we had the confidence, my goodness, of a Mack truck!"

As Greensboro's white residents streamed through Woolworth's, they reacted in surprisingly different ways to the presence of the four youths. Predictably, some heaped curses on them. Others tried to "help" the youths follow the old racist ways, pointing out that they did not belong in a whites-only area. But a pair of elderly white women patted them on the back. "Ah," said one of them, "you should have done it 10 years ago."

The students were not served that day, but back on campus, they discovered they had become heroes. Their protest had lifted them above the status of straight-A students, above even the hero worship enjoyed by the college's top football stars. And A & T's president, a black administrator previously noted for his meek obedience to white authorities, reacted to the sit-in with unexpected sympathy. The reasons for targeting Woolworth's puzzled him, he said—the store had never had a reputation for good food—but he did not order the students disciplined. Their protest soon inspired followers. One student described the rush to the lunch counter: "It was like a fever. Everyone wanted to go. We were so happy."

The next day, 20 other A & T students joined the first group. On the fourth day, white students from the University of North Carolina Women's College in Greensboro entered the protest. Next, the sit-ins spread to half a dozen towns around the state. The new targets included shopping centers, drugstores, theaters, drive-ins, and other public places. As the movement widened, reporters began querying Blair, Richmond, McCain, and McNeil. "How long have you been planning this?" they asked. The students' answer spoke for a whole generation of young blacks: "All our lives!"

The barriers that the students had begun to assault—barriers that kept some 19 million black Americans from full enjoyment of their citizenship—stood on a tradition more than 300 years old. Until the Civil War ended in 1865, nine of every 10 blacks in America were slaves, most of them living in the South. But the liberating of the Confederacy's blacks did not free the nation from racism; on the contrary, the seeds of prejudice flourished in the defeated South's bitter soil. Among its ugliest manifestations were the Jim Crow laws aimed at keeping dark-skinned Americans a separate, humble, and powerless minority.

Daily humiliations of blacks were limited only by a southern community's imagination. In 1905, for example, Georgia passed a law barring blacks and whites from using the same park facilities; donors of land for playgrounds had to specify which race could use them. Until 1940 blacks and whites in Atlanta were not allowed to visit the city zoo at the same time. In 1915 Oklahoma required separate telephone booths for white and black callers. A 1922 Mississippi

Travelers congregate at a train station in Jacksonville, Florida, in the 1920s. Before the civil rights movement, black passengers at this depot— as at others throughout the South—could use only facilities marked Colored.

statute forbade different races to share taxis except in intercity travel. Many public libraries permitted the mingling of black and white only on the pages of books; their buildings were reserved for whites. Separate Bibles for courtroom oaths, separate doors, separate elevators and stairways, separate drinking fountains, and separate toilets existed even where not required by law.

In mid-20th-century America, Jim Crow extended in every direction. Blacks attended separate and inferior schools, sat in the rear seats of buses, and knew better than to ask for service at white-owned restaurants or hotels. Whites used rest rooms marked "Men" and "Women"; blacks followed signs for "Colored." Southerners usually offered blacks back entrances to public buildings, but seldom *any* entrance to voting booths. Racist officials—backed by Jim Crow laws and assisted by fear of lynchings, or mob murders—discouraged blacks from engaging in political activity. Even in death, not all were equal: cemeteries were racially segregated, along with funeral notices in many local papers (white deaths were routinely reported on top, black deaths below).

As the 20th century advanced, millions of landless southern black laborers fled the farms and plantations for better-paying jobs in the cities. This migration made for hard adjustments, but it gave blacks more freedom to organize, to become educated, and to develop a small middle class, all of which encouraged hopes of rising further in American society. Many blacks settled in the North, where for the first time they could vote without fear of racial violence. As candidates from both major parties campaigned for their support, the importance of civil rights as a national issue also grew.

Foreign challenges further contributed to the country's growing tolerance. From 1941 to 1945, the war against Nazi Germany, whose leaders murdered millions of Jews and other peoples branded as "inferior," helped awaken Americans to the dangers of racial ideology. Soon after the war ended, when the United States and the Soviet Union began to compete for the favor of rising nonwhite nations in Asia and Africa, racism became a damaging embarrassment to America, a nation that claimed to stand for freedom and democracy.

In 1954 the leading civil rights organization, the National Association for the Advancement of Colored People (NAACP), advanced these changes by winning *Brown v. Board of Education of Topeka*, a

Thurgood Marshall (fourth from right), special counsel for the National Association for the Advancement of Colored People (NAACP), joins his colleagues outside the U.S. Supreme Court building in May 1954. The team of attorneys had just successfully argued Brown v. Board of Education of Topeka, *the historic case that ended legal school segregation.*

landmark Supreme Court case that outlawed segregation in public schools. The Court's ruling encouraged African Americans to stage bolder protests against Jim Crow, including a yearlong 1956 boycott that helped end segregation on buses in Montgomery, Alabama.

The bus boycott brought national fame to its young leader, Dr. Martin Luther King, Jr. To draw attention to the evils of segregation, King urged blacks to refuse to cooperate with a racist system, even to the point of disobeying Jim Crow laws and accepting jail. Yet as a minister who called for nonviolence in thought and deed, King reassured whites even as he inspired blacks. So, too, did his descriptions of the protest in Montgomery as a struggle not against whites but against injustice.

But King knew that for all the media attention, the Montgomery boycott had affected only a single bus company in a single city. To cripple Jim Crow, the struggle would have to involve blacks throughout the South. King also understood that this would require support from the churches, which were not simply places of worship but also the main centers of community life for southern blacks.

In January 1957, King welcomed 60 southern black leaders to Atlanta, Georgia, where they formed a network of local groups devoted to applying "nonviolent direct action" against Jim Crow. The new organization became known as the Southern Christian Leadership Conference (SCLC). The group's title reflected the fact that most of the delegates were

Pictured with fellow clergymen (left to right) Theodore J. Jemison, C. K. Steele, and Fred L. Shuttlesworth, Martin Luther King, Jr., leads a discussion on desegregation in Atlanta, Georgia. Such dialogues laid the groundwork for King's Southern Christian Leadership Conference, the civil rights organization he founded in 1957.

ministers; because black ministers drew their salaries wholly from their congregations, not white employers, they had the financial independence to lead protests against racism.

The fledgling SCLC elected King as its first president. He soon began planning a Washington, D.C., rally to urge Congressional passage of a black voting-rights bill. Roy Wilkins of the NAACP, a group that preferred quiet legal efforts to mass action, backed the rally after King agreed to soften its tone, even calling it a "Prayer Pilgrimage" instead of a protest. Held on May 17, 1957, the event drew some 25,000 people, whom King roused with the cry, "Give us the ballot!"

Later that year, prodded by the SCLC and the NAACP, Congress passed the Civil Rights Act, a mild measure but the first law in nearly a century aimed at the protection of black civil rights. By the time the bill had slowly wound its way through Congress, however, determined southern senators had managed to kill most of its key features. In particular, they insisted that any official charged with violating black voting rights be tried by a local jury—which, in the South, meant almost certain acquittal by 12 local whites. Still, NAACP leader Roy Wilkins reluctantly accepted this "crumb from Congress" as a small step on a long uphill journey toward racial equality.

Just how steep this climb would be became clear later in September 1957 when a federal court ordered public schools in Little Rock, Arkansas, to begin accepting blacks. Arkansas governor Orval Faubus responded by sending the state National Guard to Central High School to keep black students from entering on opening day. Faubus's action encouraged mobs to form outside the school, where they taunted and menaced the black children trying to go to their classes.

White students taunt Elizabeth Eckford as she tries to enter Central High School in Little Rock, Arkansas, on September 6, 1957. When a federal judge ordered Little Rock public schools to admit blacks, Arkansas governor Orval Faubus sent National Guardsmen to block their path.

President Dwight D. Eisenhower countered by sending 1,000 troops from the crack 101st Airborne Division to Little Rock. By 5:00 A.M. paratroopers with fixed bayonets had ringed the school. Several hours later, nine black children arrived in an army station wagon and filed past their armed escort to their first experience with integrated education. But instead of becoming more active for civil rights after this incident, Eisenhower decided, along with much of the nation, that local race relations were best left alone.

It was three years later, in 1960—the same year the Greensboro students made their historic stand at the Woolworth's lunch counter—that a young American athlete felt the shocking sting of Jim Crow's venom. Contending at the 1960 Olympic Games, held that year in Rome, Italy, was an 18-year-old light heavyweight boxer out of Louisville, Kentucky. The youth battled a Polish champion in Rome, won a unanimous 5–0 decision, collected a dazzling Olympic gold medal, and returned to a hero's welcome. His hometown gave him a parade and a party attended by congratulatory celebrities, including the governor of Kentucky and the mayor of Louisville. When the young champion went to a local restaurant afterward, however, employees refused to serve him because he was black. Disgusted by the country he had just proudly represented abroad, Cassius Clay—soon to be known as Muhammad Ali, heavyweight champion of the world—threw his Olympic gold medal into the Ohio River.

Such incidents, multiplied by the thousands and punctuated by Little Rock and other national clashes, combined to create a new understanding for many blacks: if they wanted to give practical meaning to the actions of Congress and the courts, they would have to challenge Jim Crow on their own.

In the sit-ins that began to sweep the South, young blacks took the lead, at times working in NAACP youth chapters that showed far more enthusiasm for "nonviolent direct action" than the group's national office. The younger generation of black Americans had become wholly impatient with the pace of civil rights progress. Raised on the promise of the *Brown* case and the Montgomery bus boycott, they awaited only a spark to ignite an all-out attack on Jim Crow. Their ideas on precisely how to act were still taking shape, but they had no doubts about the goal—to express fully the ideals of American democracy.

2

THE SIT-INS SPREAD

ALL across America, black youths strained for details of the Greensboro protests—as if they were listening to news about their own future. Cleveland Sellers, then a 16-year-old South Carolina high school honors student, recalled that word of the sit-ins hit him "like a shot of adrenaline" and left him with "a burning desire to get involved." In Atlanta, 17-year-old Ruby Doris Smith ran home from Spelman College to catch television coverage of the sit-in, and began thinking that perhaps this could happen in her city, too. A brooding 26-year-old high school teacher in New York City, Robert Moses, stared at a newspaper picture of the Greensboro youths and felt a strange closeness. He found on their faces a certain look—"angry, determined"—that was unlike the fearful, timid expressions he had seen on the faces of so many southern blacks.

Within months of the first sit-in, Sellers was leading protests in his small hometown, Smith had joined

A lone black student stages a March 1960 sit-in at a Nashville, Tennessee, lunch counter. Employees refused to serve him and, to discourage others from following his lead, covered the remaining stools with packages.

Picketing in front of a New York City Woolworth's store, union members demonstrate their support for the North Carolina sit-in movement.

a campaign in Atlanta, and Moses was heading south to give his full time to the student movement. They were among hundreds, then thousands, of young blacks from different backgrounds who challenged the color line, all of them certain that the actions of those

four freshmen in Greensboro had something to do
with their own lives.

The rising tide of protest needed less than a week
to spill over state borders into Virginia and South
Carolina. One week more and whites in Chattanooga

The son of Alabama sharecroppers and a firm believer in the power of "soul force," John Robert Lewis would become a central figure in the civil rights battles of the 1960s.

and Nashville, Tennessee, were coping with sit-in campaigns. Over in Little Rock, Arkansas, black students started wearing badges advertising a boycott of stores that segregated blacks. "I am wearing 1959 clothes," they read, "with 1960 dignity." By the end of February, the protests had moved into the Deep South, including Montgomery, the city where Dr. King's nonviolent leadership had first commanded national attention.

In the North, blacks and whites supported the sit-ins by refusing to buy goods at Woolworth's and other chain stores whose southern branches would not serve blacks at lunch counters. These "sympathy boy-cotts" gained wide backing and made clear to store executives that racial discrimination was going to cost them a great deal of money.

In some northern stores, employees greeted pro-testers with enthusiasm. At one New York City Wool-worth's, for example, a man with a Bible concession in the store told a protester, "You're losing me business like crazy—but don't stop. I'd even join you if I didn't have my concession here." Returning to his counter, he said softly, "I guess people have been reading my product lately."

The spreading protests raised up new leaders to inspire the student movement. As young blacks sought guiding principles for their actions, they paid special attention to a group of demonstrators in Nash-ville. Unlike the college freshmen whose act of naive courage first sparked the sit-ins, the Nashville protest-ers were somewhat older students or graduates who had held their first workshop in the nonviolent ideals of King a year before the Greensboro sit-in.

Among the Nashville students whose lives re-vealed the religious roots of student activism, John Robert Lewis was one of the most determined. Hu-morous but intense, Lewis was one of 10 children born to sharecroppers in rural Alabama. The Christian piety of his family and neighbors moved him, and he began preaching at the age of four to the family chickens and then duly baptizing them. In high school, classmates had dubbed him "Preacher" for his Sunday sermons at nearby churches. Lewis would listen to radio sermons by Martin Luther King, Jr., in the days before the Montgomery boycott. He admired King for using the emotional power of the Negro church to inspire blacks to seek freedom in a spirit of love and nonviolence.

Other Nashville students shared Lewis's belief that religious idealism could overcome racism, not with physical strength but with "soul force." Their aim was to build a "Beloved Community" of all people, based on harmony and equality. This ideal gave them the faith and courage to risk beatings and jail in order to help America become a land of full justice and opportunity.

An equally well known, though very different, student group operated in the "Queen City of the South," Atlanta. Here, in the region's largest, wealthiest city, lived its richest, most powerful black community. Here, too, were many of the country's most talented and ambitious black college students. They gathered at Atlanta University, a sprawling network of six campuses that centered on Morehouse College (King's alma mater), known as the black Harvard, and its sister school, Spelman College.

The Atlanta students were not especially devoted to the spiritual side of the sit-in movement, but they inspired others in more down-to-earth ways: as a group, they were expected to become professional and business leaders in black communities across the country, but they risked their safe career paths by joining the lunch counter sit-ins. This commitment reflected their faith that the sit-ins would soon topple the one great barrier to success and dignity—the color line. This hopeful, joyous mood perfectly suited a generation of African Americans fired by a growing confidence in their abilities and their future in American society.

The protests in Atlanta began with student Lonnie King, a powerfully built former navy recruit and star football running back. Aware that his background as a child of the slums and former boxer (and brawler) might limit his appeal to the elegant and refined students of Atlanta University, he looked for a student ally with a gift for words and the right touch of sophistication. Striding into the university's student hangout, Yates and Milton's drugstore, King happened to spot Julian Bond, the handsome, popular, 20-year-old son of an eminent scholar and college dean, who had already gained fame for publishing two poems on black American life.

Lonnie King held out a newspaper with the headline, GREENSBORO STUDENT SIT-IN, THIRD DAY. "Have you seen that?" King asked.

"Yeah, you know, I read the papers," Bond replied cautiously.

"What do you think about it?" pressed King.

Georgia state legislator Julian Bond holds a 1966 news conference in Atlanta. Six years earlier, he and a group of fellow students had landed in jail for trying to use the public cafeteria in Atlanta's city hall.

"Well, it's all right, pretty good stuff," his friend answered.

"Don't you think it ought to happen here?" King asked.

"It probably will," said Bond.

"Let's make it happen!" King urged.

Bond would recall thinking, "What do you mean, let *us?*" But as he later said, "You know, Lonnie's a very persuasive guy." The two young men agreed to walk through the drugstore and call students to a noon meeting about organizing new sit-ins. Lonnie King had just found his ally, and Atlanta University had just gained its protest leadership.

The next move offered a remarkable display of student planning and organization. At precisely 11:00 A.M. on March 15, 1960, 200 Atlanta students simultaneously marched on 10 different eating places. The youths focused on government-owned property and public places that might be expected to serve all comers: bus and train stations, the state capitol, and the Federal Building. Determined to use the municipal cafeteria, Julian Bond led about a dozen students to City Hall. Public Is Welcome, they read on the large sign in front of the building. And so they entered, the young men wearing neckties, the young women dressed as if for a church social. Then the expected clash took place.

The heavyset cafeteria manager approached the students. "Well, we can't serve you here," she said sternly. "That's not true," one of the students replied. "You've got a sign outside saying the public is welcome and we're the public and we want to eat." But the manager did not appear to be interested in this logic. She quickly telephoned the lieutenant governor, who sent a squad of policemen to the scene in a patrol wagon. The officers carted the students off and deposited them at the jail known as Big Rock.

In the Deep South of the 1960s, being arrested was alarming for any black. For the relatively privileged students of Atlanta University, it was not only frightening but distressingly unfamiliar; before the Greensboro sit-in, being in jail would have been un-thinkable. Trying to calm his fellow students, Bond kept telling them they would all be out in 15 minutes, but most remained apprehensive. Their inexperience with the legal system took its toll in several directions. In court, for example, the judge asked Bond how he wanted to plead. "How do I plead?" Bond whispered to his attorney. "Innocent, you fool!" bellowed the lawyer.

Innocence did not greatly help the students; the judge sent them back to jail on a variety of trumped-up charges. One charge was for violating an 1870s law intended to stop meetings by the Ku Klux Klan; now this same law was being used to punish blacks who had gathered to request service in a cafeteria.

Jail proved a crucial test of student commitment. "We've been here about six hours," students complained to Bond. "You said we were getting out in about an hour." Replying as casually as he could, Bond said, "Don't worry about it, fellas, we'll be out in a minute." But it was many hours later when the students' parents arrived at the jail with bail money. Now, for these unlikely ex-prisoners, inner doubt suddenly turned to open pride. In high spirits, they poured into the halls of Spelman College, where, as Bond jokingly noted later, "they could be heroes, you know, with the women."

For most of these heroes, it had been their first and last time in jail. But it had been enough to make them realize that, if it meant standing up nonviolently for their civil rights, jail could be a badge of honor for even the most proper blacks. No longer content to attend the best segregated college in the country, the students now examined the exciting notion that transforming society must be their first order of business.

Other signs, too, gave young blacks hope for an end to second-class citizenship. In New York City, for example, Lorraine Hansberry's play about black ghetto life, A *Raisin in the Sun*, had premiered on Broadway in March 1959. The drama, starring Claudia McNeil, Ruby Dee, and Sidney Poitier, was directed by Lloyd Richards, Broadway's first black director in more than half a century. Opening to rave reviews, *Raisin* won the coveted Drama Critics Circle Award and enjoyed the longest Broadway run up to that time of any play by a black author.

Those involved in *Raisin in the Sun* went on to further successes, including the filmed version of the play. Poitier became the first black in cinema history to win the Academy Award for Best Actor. He won for his performance in 1963's *Lilies of the Field*, a joyous film that showed how deep friendships can develop across racial lines. McNeil went on to a long subsequent career in Hollywood and on Broadway and television. She received the London Critics Poll best actress award for her role in James Baldwin's *The Amen Corner* in 1965.

Dee, a tall, commanding presence on stage, became the first black actress to appear at the American Shakespeare Festival, won the 1966 Drama Desk Award for playing the lead in black playwright Alice Childress's *Wedding Band*, and earned an Obie for her work in South African playwright Athol Fugard's *Boesman and Lena* in 1971. Hansberry, who died of cancer at the age of 34 in 1965, also wrote *The Sign in Sidney Brustein's Window*, a 1964 Broadway play, along with numerous essays and film adaptations. Her work marked an important milestone for black artists in the professional theater.

As student protests continued to spread, white hostility increased. When the city of Huntsville, Alabama, experienced its first sit-in, many white residents felt genuine puzzlement, believing until then that race relations had been fine. But the lunch counter sit-ins alerted whites that they had been enjoying a period of silent surrender to racist laws, not real harmony. When blacks began expressing their grievances openly, the mood in Huntsville turned bitter.

Young civil rights workers found that the Woolworth's lunch counter in Huntsville served mainly harassment. That, however, was mild compared with the fare at a nearby Walgreen's drugstore, where the police seized protesting students. At the county jail, fingerprinting and the taking of mug shots informed the students that Huntsville's police viewed them as common criminals. One of the young women wrote about her time in jail: "Ten of us girls were placed in a cell. . . . We slept on the floor. Supper was over when we got there; there was no food until breakfast time: 5:30 A.M. We girls found the biscuits, gravy and stewed peaches not too appetizing so we didn't eat. The boys 'dug in' as only boys can."

The police arrested dozens of students on any excuse. They hauled in one student who had accidentally brushed arms with an officer; the charge was assault and battery. Police also began looking the other way when white residents of Huntsville beat blacks who participated in the sit-ins. In one attack whites burned three protesters (also white) with oil of mustard, a highly irritating substance that gave its name to the German poison gas of World War I.

The deterioration of race relations in Huntsville was typical of many communities in which blacks and white sympathizers protested against Jim Crow. In Nashville, whites pushed lighted cigarettes against the backs of girls sitting at a lunch counter. The Ku Klux Klan pistol-whipped a 16-year-old in Jacksonville, Florida, also the site of a never-punished murder: a

Attempting to integrate a lunch counter in Jackson, Mississippi, in 1960, an interracial trio of protesters gamely ignores a barrage of abuse.

black man who had nothing to do with the demonstrations but who drove through a police roadblock was shot dead by a white service-station attendant. In Biloxi, Mississippi, a white mob shot and wounded 10 blacks at a public beach.

Students reeled from the beatings, mass arrests, and constant insults, but the sit-in movement as a whole drew strength from such suffering. If some students had begun the protests in the spirit of a lark, the ordeal of white violence now pushed them toward a more mature, carefully thought-out commitment. For students who had suffered mob violence and hostility from police and judges, the originally vague ideals of nonviolence and the "Beloved Community" suddenly took on clear and powerful meaning.

The protesters drew on their religious faith to carry them through the harsh times. Old spirituals referring to freedom lent the power of black cultural tradition to the sit-in campaigns. And the students themselves created songs to express their faith, in their country as well as their god. Three young women serving 49 days in a Florida jail for sitting in at a Woolworth's lunch counter created "Fight On," a soon-to-be-popular song that blended an element of the spiritual with the nonviolent principles of King, seasoned with a touch of American political idealism:

> Gone to the jail, without paying our bail
> Justice will come right over the trail. . . .
> We're fighting, we're fighting, for a better land we know.
> For the Constitution tells us so
> Fight on, fight on.

Of the many songs, one stood out for its haunting melody and simple faith in God and man. Slaves had sung it as a spiritual, and it had boosted the spirits of striking black tobacco workers in the Carolinas during the 1940s. In the late 1950s white folksingers strummed the tune at Tennessee's famed Highlander Folk School, a place that welcomed civil rights workers, union organizers, and good music with equal enthusiasm. After some of the musicians reworked it to restore its original free-spirited Baptist flavor, it became "We Shall Overcome," the civil rights movement's most powerful anthem.

Defying insults, beatings, and terror tactics, the movement's young protesters maintained their commitment to nonviolence, sometimes even impressing diehard segregationists. Many students based their rules of nonviolent behavior on the writings of such spiritual leaders as Martin Luther King, Jr. Others invented their own codes of dignified conduct on the spot. One day in Atlanta, for example, the manager

Civil rights activists James Bevel (center) and Fred Shuttlesworth (right) meet with other political reformers in 1961 at the Highlander Folk School in Monteagle, Tennessee. It was at Highlander that musicians revised the old hymn "We Shall Overcome," and made it the era's most powerful anthem.

of a department store lunchroom quietly walked up behind the stool where Spelman College student Lana Taylor waited for service. As shocked white patrons and young demonstrators looked on, the manager grabbed the delicate-looking young black woman by the shoulders, cursed her, and ordered her out of the store. It was a miscalculation on his part—and a moment that marked the character of a movement.

"Lana was not going," recalled a young white witness. "She put her hands under the counter and held. He was rough and strong. She just held and I looked down at that moment at her hands . . . brown, strained . . . every muscle holding. . . . All of a sudden he let go and left. I thought he knew he could not move that girl—ever."

The spring of 1960 saw local merchants make the first concessions to the sit-in protesters. Although in some cities violence was the rule, in others—those in which merchants and politicians demanded booming business and racial peace—peaceful agreements prevailed. By the summer, more than 30 southern cities, including 12 in Florida, had set up community organizations to act on local blacks' complaints of discrimination. Young protesters took special satisfaction from the news, on July 25, 1960, that Woolworth's lunch counters would begin serving blacks in Greensboro, North Carolina.

By that fall, the outlines of an enduring student movement were clearly visible. To the dismay of white merchants, many of the sit-in campaigns that had quieted during the summer vacation revived in September. The following month, Atlanta University hosted 140 delegates of the Student Nonviolent Coordinating Committee (known by its initials, SNCC, and pronounced Snick), an interracial group that had risen from the southern sit-in movement. Its first permanent chairman was a black convert to Judaism named Charles McDew. He explained his involvement in the protests against racial injustice by quoting the first-century Jewish sage Hillel. His words might have served as SNCC's answer to pleas by whites (and some older blacks) for patience and restraint:

> If I am not for myself, then who is for me?
> If I am for myself alone, then what am I?
> If not now, when?

At the SNCC convention in Atlanta, McDew pledged that the protests would continue until "every vestige of racial segregation and discrimination is erased from the face of the earth." Determined that no part of American life would long remain beyond their supremely confident reach, young blacks cheered McDew's call for new and greater nonviolent campaigns.

3

THE FREEDOM RIDES

Bᴸᴬᶜᴷ protest in 1960, a presidential election year, led candidates of both the Democratic and Republican parties to declare their commitment to the cause of racial equality. Their campaign pledges encouraged blacks to believe that the next president would be a strong ally in their struggle for equal rights. The Democratic nominee, Senator John F. Kennedy, did the most to touch the imagination of African Americans with his calls for a "New Frontier" of bold reform, a vision that fit well with hopes for stronger leadership on civil rights.

The sensitive subject of the sit-ins gave Kennedy a chance to stand apart from the caution of other politicians. Kennedy praised the sit-ins as showing that the American spirit was "coming alive again." The goals of the sit-ins, he declared, deserved the support of the government as well as of individuals. To those who had doubts about the wisdom of these protests, Kennedy added, "It is in the American tradition to stand up for one's rights—even if the new way is to sit down."

The Republican candidate, Richard M. Nixon, also declared his support for civil rights. Both he and Kennedy faced the greatest test of their commitments

Dazed Freedom Riders watch helplessly as their bus, gutted by a white mob in May 1961, burns to ashes near Anniston, Alabama. Commenting on such episodes, civil rights leader James Farmer observed, "If any man says he had no fear in the action of the sixties, he is a liar."

when Martin Luther King, Jr., was arrested at a protest in Atlanta on October 19. King was then sentenced, on a minor charge, to four months of hard labor in a distant rural prison. His wife, Coretta, feared that he might never get out of prison alive.

Nixon, who had a solid record of support for civil rights, considered expressing sympathy for King, but his worries about losing southern white voters led him to keep silent. Kennedy followed a more active course. No one on his staff was sure of the political effects—would this help him with blacks or simply hurt him with whites?—but on the urging of close aides, he followed his inclination and called Coretta King on October 26 to assure her of his support.

Kennedy's forceful younger brother and campaign manager, Robert, meanwhile telephoned the judge who had sentenced King. No one knows just what was said, but "Bobby" Kennedy made clear his strong belief that King should be freed. The next morning, acting under what he later admitted was considerable pressure, the judge ordered King released.

At first the impact of Kennedy's actions on the white South seemed so uncertain that the candidate avoided public statements about his efforts for King. But the story of King's release gained wide attention among black Americans. The Democratic party helped spread the good news in black neighborhoods with a pamphlet that compared "A Candidate with a Heart, Senator Kennedy" with "'No Comment' Nixon." King himself had remained officially neutral about the election, but after learning of Kennedy's aid he showered the Democratic candidate with praise.

Kennedy squeaked to victory. Any of several ethnic and religious groups might have claimed credit for his success, but the black vote was undeniably crucial: some 70 percent of all black ballots went to Kennedy, helping him win key northern states along with Texas and South Carolina. Many African Americans, including Martin Luther King, Jr., expressed their hope that Kennedy's election would also prove a victory for the cause of racial equality.

Kennedy had stirred hopes for change during his campaign, and he raised those hopes further with a memorable inaugural address. Although he did not specifically mention racial issues, black Americans drew hope from his focus on defending "human rights, to which this nation has always been committed, and to which we are committed today at home and around the world." The president urged people everywhere to "ask what together we can do for the freedom of man." Civil rights leaders rejoiced as they prepared to ask this question more boldly in the years ahead.

Early in his administration, Kennedy took several steps to promote black rights. The most visible change was an immediate rise in the number of blacks appointed to government posts. Not long after taking office, he appointed Harvard Ph.D. and housing expert Robert Weaver as administrator of the Federal Housing and Home Finance Agency, the highest federal post so far ever held by a black. Another "first" occurred in 1961, when Kennedy named a 50-year-old Chicago attorney, James B. Parsons, to the District Court of Northern Illinois, making him the first black federal judge in the continental United States.

These federal appointments seemed to inspire similar moves at the state level. The year 1962, for example, produced several significant milestones in black American history. First, Boston lawyer Edward W. Brooke won election as attorney general for Massachusetts, making him New England's highest-ranking black official. Next, Georgia elected its first black state legislator since Reconstruction, the era that followed the South's defeat in the Civil War: Leroy Johnson, an attorney from Atlanta, won a seat in the Georgia State Senate. The year also saw the arrival in Washington, D.C., of Augustus Hawkins, the first black ever to represent the state of California in the U.S. Congress.

The nation's black community looked approvingly at several steps taken by Kennedy. He directed that federal funds should not be spent in any way that encouraged discrimination, a clear message to corporations that did business with the government: hire qualified blacks. Government leaders also welcomed African Americans in White House social circles, and many officials resigned from clubs that refused membership to blacks. Such gestures were valued by civil rights leaders who believed that commitment to racial equality should begin at home—especially when that home was the White House. But for all the signs of change, Kennedy failed to do nearly as much as black leaders were expecting. Because he faced strong opposition even to some of his minor bills, and because he feared offending powerful southern senators at the beginning of his term, the president chose not to sponsor a strong civil rights measure. He won praise for naming 53-year-old NAACP chief counsel Thurgood Marshall to an important federal judiciary position (associate judge on the Second Circuit Court of Appeals, with jurisdiction over New York, Connecticut, and Vermont) in 1961. But he also bowed to powerful Senator James Eastland from Mississippi, nominating a judge who soon proved as bitterly opposed to integration as Eastland himself.

Kennedy's early civil rights record disappointed black leaders mainly because he himself had encouraged such high hopes. Most blacks still believed in Kennedy's sincerity and in the possibilities for continued progress toward equality. They also believed that he could do better. And with growing pressure from civil rights groups, they concluded, he would.

In the spring of 1961, a small, nonviolent protest group called the Congress of Racial Equality (CORE) moved into the national spotlight. CORE chief James

Under arrest for breaking Mississippi segregation laws, James Farmer, 41-year-old director of the Congress of Racial Equality, marches out of the Jackson bus station in 1961. Farmer and a group of young volunteers were headed for the Hinds County Prison Farm, an institution notorious—even in Mississippi—for its brutality to blacks.

Farmer outlined plans for a series of interracial "Freedom Rides" on public buses throughout the Deep South. The project's stated mission was to test southern acceptance of a recent Supreme Court ban on segregation in long-distance bus terminals. But CORE volunteers had another, riskier goal as well: to expose acts of racial violence in the South, thereby spurring the federal government to protect black rights more vigorously.

Farmer came to this campaign a respected veteran of civil rights protest. In 1942, he had been instrumental in founding CORE and establishing its firm commitment to civil rights and integration, both among its own members and in the wider society. Farmer, a stout man with a deep, powerful voice and a hearty laugh, believed in nonviolence, but he also believed in the value of confrontation in advancing civil rights. He explained the idea behind the Freedom Rides: "We put on pressure and create a crisis" for government leaders "and then they react."

Traveling in two buses—one Greyhound, one Trailways—seven black and six white volunteers left Washington, D.C., on May 4, 1961. The travelers were bound for Alabama and Mississippi, states known both for their rigid Jim Crow traditions and for their willingness to back up those traditions with police and mob violence. Most of the black volunteers (all men) had participated in sit-ins, and the whites (three women, three men) had worked for world peace and other causes. Yet all of them understood that the risks of making this bus trip were beyond anything they had ever experienced.

John Lewis, one of the 13 volunteers, probably summed up the feelings of his fellow riders when he said he would "give up all if necessary for the Freedom Ride" because human dignity was "the most important thing" in his life. He came close to doing just that at the Greyhound terminal in Rock Hill, South Carolina, when he tried to enter the white rest room. He explained his constitutional rights to what he later described as "several young white hoodlums" with "leather jackets, ducktail haircuts, standing there smoking," who blocked his way. When he tried to walk past, they clubbed him to the ground. Several more incidents of violence or harassment occurred as the bus wound its way south. Then it entered Alabama, and the riders braced for greater danger.

On May 14, the lead bus moved into Anniston, where residents lined the streets in expectation of the "Yankee troublemakers." To Genevieve Hughes, one of the young riders, it seemed that everyone in the town was concentrating on making them feel unwelcome: "The mob was out. . . . They walked by the side of the bus carrying sticks and metal bars."

With no policemen to protect the riders and keep the peace, local anger soon flared into violence. Vigilantes slit two tires on the bus and tossed rocks at the windows. The bus left Anniston soon afterward, with 40 cars chasing close behind, but when the two slashed tires went flat, the bus stopped again and the pursuers resumed their work of smashing the windows. Then, screaming obscenities and holding pipes and chains, they tried to storm the bus.

Eli Cowling, a white southerner who had boarded the bus in Atlanta, quickly responded to the assault. Moving to the door with a pistol in his hand, he held back the mob for more than 15 minutes. Everyone on both sides assumed that the heroic Cowling was an ordinary passenger, but in fact he was a state highway patrolman who had come on orders of Alabama's chief official. Governor John Patterson had done his best to whip up public rage against the Freedom Riders, but he still wanted to avoid the bad publicity that was bound to explode if a mass killing of travelers occurred in his state.

Passengers huddled inside the bus until, as Genevieve Hughes recalled, a man "thrust a bundle, seemingly of rags, through the window opposite me, at the same time lighting it. There was a noise, sparks flew and a dense cloud of smoke immediately filled the bus. I thought it was only a smoke bomb and climbed over the back of the seat. The smoke became denser and denser, becoming completely black."

Then Hughes and other passengers saw flames shooting from the bus and realized it was a firebomb. Hughes thought they were all going to die. The riders dashed outside, some scrambling through the holes where bus windows had been. Men from the mob charged the dazed passengers and had begun to beat them when a gunshot froze them in place. Eli Cowling

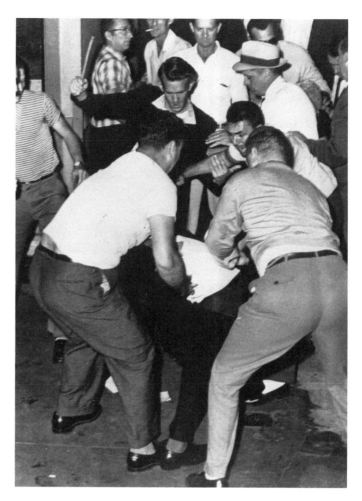

Armed with lead pipes and baseball bats, Alabamians attack a Freedom Rider at the Birmingham bus station on May 14, 1961. Although informed of the violence, Police Chief Eugene "Bull" Connor made no effort to stop it.

warned that he would kill the next person who hit anyone. The mob melted away. Shaken riders regrouped across the street, and the people on whose lawn they were standing came out to offer a different kind of southern welcome. "It's a shame," said one resident, and invited the travelers inside. Meanwhile, state troopers could be seen conversing just as warmly with the mob leaders.

Later that day, the second bus also came under attack at Anniston, but it reached the Birmingham terminal on schedule. There, passengers found a waiting gang of 30 heavyset young men armed with baseball bats, lead pipes, and bicycle chains. Having earlier been secretly encouraged by the chief of police, Eugene "Bull" Connor, the mob lit into the riders. The beatings were so violent that an FBI informant on the scene reported that he "couldn't see [the victims'] faces through the blood." Afterward reporters swarmed around Chief Connor to ask why no police had been stationed at the terminal. It was Mother's Day, Connor solemnly reminded them, so naturally, no officers were available.

The riders continued on to Montgomery. On the morning of May 20, 1961, John Lewis found Alabama's capital city strangely quiet, resembling "a ghost town. . . . You couldn't see any other buses." Nor any police. Once again the group's travel plans had been publicized to hostile whites. When the riders got out of the bus, people suddenly rushed at them from the surrounding buildings. Lewis saw his briefcase ripped from his grasp and torn to shreds before someone struck him in the head with a wooden soda crate. When he regained consciousness, a man was standing over him to serve a state court order forbidding integrated travel in Alabama.

A high-ranking aide to Robert Kennedy, now the nation's attorney general, was monitoring events in the Montgomery bus terminal when the violence exploded. Spotting two young women being assaulted by the mob, he shouted, "I'm a federal man!" and tried to escort them from the area. But the idea of federal officials involving themselves in local race relations did not go down well in white Alabama. Local thugs clubbed the Kennedy aide from behind, then left him bleeding on the pavement, where he lay unattended for nearly half an hour.

Later that evening the battered Freedom Riders took refuge at a black church in Montgomery. There, they heard Martin Luther King, Jr., preach on the justice of their cause. Outside an angry mob torched

Demonstrators wait out a night of terror at a church in Montgomery, Alabama, in May 1961. Outside, federal marshals barely managed to keep a shrieking mob from setting fire to the crowded church.

a car and tossed tear gas bombs through the church's stained glass windows. There were shouted calls to burn down the church, but then federal marshals began to arrive. To avoid offending whites suspicious of federal interference in their communities, the marshals carried no firearms, but they managed to keep the mob away from the church until the Alabama National Guard took over. This move probably saved the lives of the 1,200 people trapped inside.

The Kennedys now publicly pressed civil rights leaders for a "cooling off" period, fearing that more rides might bring still worse violence. But black leaders insisted on continuing. James Farmer's response was terse: "We had been cooling off for 100 years. If we got any cooler, we'd be in a deep freeze."

Unable to stop the rides and unwilling either to send troops or to let the riders face possible death through mob assault, the Kennedys turned to Senator James Eastland of Mississippi to keep the peace. As riders prepared to enter Eastland's home state, Robert Kennedy privately obtained the senator's promise to guarantee their safety. In return Eastland received assurances that the federal government would not oppose the arrest of the Freedom Riders. The deal held: no violence touched the rides into Mississippi, and police arrested some 300 passengers.

By late 1961, the Freedom Rides were still going on and appeared set to keep rolling without end. Robert Kennedy, eager to quiet the racial tensions that were embarrassing the government, prodded southern officials to end segregation in the bus terminals. Faced with the threat of lawsuits by the Justice Department, most southern communities took down signs for "white" and "colored" in the terminals. The larger goal of CORE—to push the president into a strong public commitment to end Jim Crow—remained a distant hope. But in late 1962 CORE was able to announce that thanks to the Freedom Rides segregation in interstate travel had ended.

Segregation in education was also reeling. Civil rights activists had been hammering on the academic world's Jim Crow for years; by 1962 the tough old specter was tottering. One of those who struck the final blows was Mississippi's James Meredith, a black nine-year veteran of the U.S. Air Force. Inspired by John F. Kennedy's January 1961 inauguration speech, Meredith had applied for entry to the historically all-white University of Mississippi—"Ole Miss" to southern loyalists.

Surrounded by sneering white students, James Meredith crosses the University of Mississippi campus in October 1962. "Ole Miss" had admitted the qualified air force veteran only after a fight involving several detachments of state troopers, 60 National Guardsmen, and 400 U.S. marshals.

"I am an American-Mississippi-Negro citizen," Meredith wrote on his application. "With all of the . . . changes in our educational system taking place, . . . I feel certain that this application does not come as a surprise to you. I certainly hope that this matter will be handled in a manner that will be complimentary to the University and to the state of Mississippi."

Ole Miss officials, however, chose to handle the matter otherwise. When the university rejected him,

Meredith went to state NAACP director Medgar
Evers, who took the university to court. Meredith, he
claimed, had been illegally refused admission to the
university because of his race.

What followed was a series of rulings, reversals,
and reversals of reversals so convoluted that, under
other circumstances, the case might have been comi-
cal. Finally, the NAACP appealed to the Supreme
Court. In September 1962, Justice Hugo Black (an

University of Mississippi chancellor J. D. Williams awards a Bachelor of Arts diploma to graduating senior James Meredith in August 1963. Meredith's successful battle to integrate the previously all-white college struck a heavy blow at Jim Crow.

Alabamian by birth) ordered the university to admit Meredith immediately. Mississippi governor Ross Barnett responded for the whole diehard South: "Never!" he shouted. "We will not surrender to the evil and illegal forces of tyranny!"

Attorney General Robert Kennedy ordered a team of federal marshals to escort Meredith when he registered at the university on September 20. Barnett met them at the door. As some 2,000 Ole Miss students sang "Glory, glory, segregation," the governor read an edict that barred Meredith from the Mississippi campus "now and forever more." Next came another lengthy set of maneuvers; Kennedy obtained court orders to admit Meredith; Mississippi's Barnett ignored them. At one point, reports historian William Manchester, Kennedy told Barnett he thought

Meredith's entry would cause the university little trouble. "Why don't you try it for six months and see how it goes?" he asked the governor. "It's best for him not to go to Ole Miss," replied Barnett. "But he *likes* Ole Miss," said Kennedy softly.

Onto the university's campus at Oxford now poured thousands of white supremacists, many of them armed with rifles, shotguns, Molotov cocktails (crude, homemade hand grenades), iron bars, and bricks. Countering them were several detachments of state troopers, 60 National Guardsmen, and 400 U.S. marshals. Forbidden by the administration to use live ammunition, Meredith's protectors could defend themselves and him only with tear gas guns. During the furious Sunday night of fighting that ensued, two men, a French reporter and an Oxford bystander, were killed, 206 marshals and guardsmen were injured by flying projectiles, and 28 suffered gunshot wounds. Toward dawn, the first units of regular army troops, reluctantly ordered by President Kennedy, arrived and began arresting riot leaders.

In the eerie calm of Monday morning, most of the mob had vanished. Three U.S. marshals accompanied Meredith into the university's administration building. By now resigned to the battle's outcome, university officials politely assisted the young black man in filling out entry forms. Three semesters later (he already had college credits from extension courses) James Meredith became the first black graduate of the University of Mississippi. Jim Crow had lost another round.

4

BIRMINGHAM

THE best-known civil rights protest of the Kennedy years began in the spring of 1963. It took place in Birmingham, Alabama, one of the South's largest and most important cities—and one of its most rigidly segregated. Despite the city's booming steel industry, most blacks could find only menial jobs. They were barred from "white" water fountains and fitting rooms. Even lunch counters remained segregated. White Birmingham was determined to act as though the South's powerful sit-in movement had never happened.

Committed to upholding Jim Crow and "white supremacy," city officials went to extremes. U.S. secretary of the interior Stewart L. Udall had ordered them to open all city parks to blacks on an equal basis: instead, Birmingham closed all its parks. City leaders even shut down the local Metropolitan Opera Company because it played to integrated audiences.

Backing up these extraordinary rules was Public Safety Commissioner "Bull" Connor, the man who had kept police out of sight while white thugs beat the first Freedom Riders in 1961. Connor's police force

A police water cannon slams young people into a wall in Birmingham, Alabama, in May 1963. A few days earlier, local blacks had held a peaceful protest meeting, so enraging Police Chief Connor that he sanctioned the use of force against the protesters.

One of King's close advisers, the Reverend Fred Shuttlesworth, tries to calm Birmingham rioters in 1963. The disturbance had started when ghetto residents learned that city police officers had roughed up nonviolent black marchers, many of them women and children.

not only terrorized civil rights workers but also punished whites who did not discriminate against blacks. Twice Connor had the manager of the city's bus terminal arrested for obeying federal orders to desegregate the facilities.

Martin Luther King, Jr., believed it crucial to overcome segregation in Birmingham. Such a victory, he reasoned, would not only encourage blacks in other places to seek their rights but spur white officials to grant them. For months, King and his staff, together with a local member of the Southern Christian Leadership Conference, the Reverend Fred Shuttlesworth,

charted plans to boycott selected downtown department stores. Popular black entertainer Harry Bela-
fonte helped King raise a large reserve fund for bailing
out civil rights workers in case Connor ordered mass
arrests of demonstrators.

King placed special importance on uniting Birmingham's blacks in support of this protest. To avoid
local black resentment over his staff of "outsiders," he
recruited 250 city residents to teach the principles of
nonviolent protest at special classes in Birmingham's
black churches. King also followed the wishes of the
city's black leadership by postponing protests until
Birmingham held its April mayoral election. This,
they felt, would help Albert Boutwell, the moderate
candidate on race issues, defeat opposition candidate
Bull Connor. Boutwell won the election, and King's
staff workers began pouring into Birmingham to chart
the most ambitious protest campaign in the civil rights
movement's history.

When antisegregation rallies began on Wednes-
day, April 3, blacks found Connor surprisingly re-
strained. Birmingham's safety director knew that the
city teemed with reporters from across the country, all
of them eager to cover the protest. If the police openly
mistreated the black marchers, the demonstrators
would get the public's sympathy. Connor therefore
kept his notorious temper in check, directing the
arrest of picketers in front of the downtown stores but
ordering his officers to avoid roughness.

Blacks briefly glimpsed the rage behind Connor's
gentle pose on Sunday afternoon, when he paraded
his snarling attack dogs in front of them. To King, it
seemed only a matter of time before Connor revealed
to the American people the true character of racism.
This was an event that Alabama officials wished to
prevent at any cost.

Eight days into the SCLC campaign, a state court
made the first move. Aiming either to stop blacks from

King gazes from his prison cell in Jefferson County Courthouse in April 1963. It was here that the civil rights leader composed his celebrated "Letter from Birmingham Jail," a passionate argument for nonviolent resistance.

seeking their civil rights or to make King appear a lawbreaker, the court issued a ban on any further demonstrations. After hard reflection, King decided to disobey the court order, which he termed unjust because its sole purpose was to prop up a racist system. But he was determined to show his respect for the principles of law even as he rejected the evils of segregation: he declared his willingness to accept the penalty for his "civil disobedience" by going to jail. Regardless of his own fate, the minister told reporters pressing around him, the nonviolent protests for black rights would continue. "Here in Birmingham," he said, "we have reached the point of no return."

On April 12 (which happened to be Good Friday), Birmingham police took King to prison, where he was held in solitary confinement for three days. But King showed that physical barriers could not silence his message. While he was in jail, a group of "liberal" white Birmingham clergymen publicly branded the protests "unwise and untimely" and praised the Birmingham police for upholding the law; King seized the moment to explain to the nation the urgent moral issues at stake.

Using scraps of paper and a smuggled pen, King responded to the ministers with "Letter from Birmingham Jail," a document that would become a staple of protest literature. In it, he outlined the pain of growing up black in America; "When you are forever fighting a denigrating sense of 'nobodyness'—then you will understand why we find it difficult to wait," he said. "There comes a time when . . . men are no longer willing to be plunged into an abyss of injustice where they experience the bleakness of corroding despair. I hope, sirs, you can understand our legitimate and unavoidable impatience."

Responding to claims that the protests were illegal, King pointed to a higher moral law based on divine justice. Freedom, he pointed out, is never simply given by the strong; it must be demanded by those who have been unfairly held down. For African Americans in the past, King noted, "wait" had always meant "never."

King's letter swept aside the charge that the protests created ill will between the races. On the contrary, King declared, the entire nonviolent movement aimed only to uncover an existing evil in order to end it. Nonviolent protests against racial segregation

merely bring to the surface the hidden tension that is already alive. We bring it out in the open, where it can be

seen and dealt with. Like a boil that can never be cured so
long as it is covered up but must be opened with all its
ugliness to the natural medicines of air and light, injustice
must be exposed, with all the tension its exposure creates,
to the light of human conscience and the air of national
opinion before it can be cured.

In churches across the country, the clergy was soon
reading King's "Letter from Birmingham Jail" to pa-
rishioners, and editors reprinted it in their newspapers
and magazines. In Washington, D.C., too, the letter
became a topic of discussion, with the president
among those most impressed by its forceful pleas for
justice. King's missive came at a time when civil rights
workers were already commanding attention but still
struggling with the public perception that they opposed "law and order." The letter did much to overcome that mistaken notion by vividly portraying the
peaceful black demonstrators as defenders of the Constitution and the human spirit.

On April 20, 1963, the state of Alabama freed
King on bail, but he learned that the demonstrations
were thinning out. Most of the adult blacks willing to
go to jail had already been arrested. James Bevel, who
had joined SCLC in 1961 fresh from the Nashville
sit-ins, suggested recruiting high school students, and
King agreed that the protests needed this dramatic
new gesture of commitment by black Americans.

Soon teenagers were crowding into the churches'
nonviolence-training meetings. So were uninvited
younger brothers and sisters who begged to march
with the rest. Many parents shuddered at the thought
of exposing their young children to Bull Connor and
his police. But King argued that no one was too young
to sacrifice for freedom in a land where blacks of any
age faced racist mistreatment. The children, too,
should march, he said.

On May 2, black children filled the streets with a
joy that seemed untouched by the danger. Connor

ordered his police officers to lock them all up, but this was not so easy. The children playfully distracted police, with decoys heading one way while larger groups of picketers marched on the downtown stores.

The youngsters could also be startlingly serious. An eight-year-old girl was walking with her mother when a policeman stopped her. "What do you want?" he demanded. Looking at the towering figure, she answered without pausing, "Freedom." More than 900 children went to jail on May 2 for that goal, and the only doubts visible were on the faces of police officers. One troubled captain said to a fellow officer, "Evans, 10 or 15 years from now, we will look back on this and we will say, 'How stupid can you be?'"

Birmingham firemen flatten black demonstrators with a water broadside. If Congress failed to move against such brutality, said noted psychologist Kenneth Clark, it would mean "we'd rather offer the Negro dogs, hoses, and nightsticks than his inherent rights."

But Connor was not among the doubting. "If you'd ask half of them what freedom means, they couldn't tell you," he scoffed. On May 3, police surrounded the Sixteenth Street Baptist Church, where 1,000 blacks had assembled. When people tried to leave the church, police struck. Using the hoses at a pressure that could take off tree bark, they blasted adults and children. The jet streams ripped their clothes and left them bloodied on the ground. Police swung nightsticks into skulls and set attack dogs loose on the panicked crowd. The animals sank their fangs into three fleeing children.

News of the violence triggered a riot by the city's poorest blacks, who threw bottles and bricks at police. These blacks had had little to do with King's nonviolent campaign, but their message sounded just as loudly to whites in Birmingham: the age of the submissive Negro was gone forever.

Connor's police became increasingly violent. When the Reverend Fred Shuttlesworth went into the black district to try to calm the rioters, a jet stream from a fire hose lifted him off the ground and hurled him against a wall of the Sixteenth Street church. He was taken away unconscious in an ambulance. Connor said he regretted missing this scene, adding, "I wish they'd carried him away in a hearse."

By this point Connor's actions for "white supremacy" no longer comforted many whites. Birmingham began to fear all-out race war. Businessmen watched in alarm as sales and profits dropped because of the boycotts, the disorder, and the violence that discouraged anyone from shopping in the downtown stores. Northern business leaders, encouraged by President Kennedy, added to the pressure on Birmingham merchants to reach an agreement with the protesters. The whites resisted, but one final jolt changed their minds.

On May 7, Birmingham's leading shopkeepers told an aide to Robert Kennedy that compromise with

the black demonstrators was out of the question. Then, as King described the scene, they stepped outside and faced the results of their stubbornness: "There were Negroes on the sidewalks, in the streets, standing, sitting in the aisles of downtown stores. There were square blocks of Negroes," a "sea of black faces." In the background they could hear such freedom songs as "We Shall Overcome."

Three days later, the merchants reached a compromise with the Southern Christian Leadership Conference. In exchange for an immediate halt to the protests, the shopkeepers would meet all demands for desegregation of their stores and the hiring of blacks during the next three months. Bull Connor quickly

Using his nightstick, a Birmingham policeman points youngsters toward a waiting paddy wagon. Black youths, Bull Connor had scoffed, "couldn't tell you what freedom means," but on May 2, 1963, more than 900 black Birmingham boys and girls demonstrated— and went to jail—for freedom.

tried to break up the pact by urging whites to boycott all businesses that agreed to desegregate. To some whites, even this did not go far enough. Two dynamite explosions destroyed the home of King's brother, a minister in Birmingham, and blew out part of a motel where King was thought to be staying. While King preached in the streets against violence, the agreement he had negotiated appeared about to collapse.

Despite King's fears and Connor's fury, after the civil rights protests Birmingham moved, however reluctantly and awkwardly, into a new era of race relations. News coverage of the protests helped push this change along by awakening Americans to the brutal treatment of black citizens. One evening the television news programs featured film of five Birmingham policemen pinning a black woman to the ground, with one officer's knee at her throat. A photograph carried on the front pages of newspapers around the world showed a huge, snarling police dog lunging at a black woman.

As Americans expressed shock and outrage at events in Birmingham (which one senator said would disgrace even the openly racist nation of South Africa), President Kennedy moved to save the agreement that King had worked out with the city's merchants. Warning that he would not permit extremists to destroy the chances for racial peace, Kennedy ordered 3,000 army troops to draw near Birmingham and prepare to take control of the Alabama National Guard. The bombings quickly stopped, and the merchants began to desegregate the fountains, rest rooms, and lunch counters in their stores, and to hire blacks for jobs once reserved for whites.

The new mayor of Birmingham, Albert Boutwell, also sensed that times were changing: he repealed the city's segregation laws. Under prodding from black leaders, he eventually opened the library, city golf courses, public buildings, and finally the schools to both races. In the nation's most segregated city, a symbol of Klan power and white resistance to racial equality, blacks had won a victory, in the Reverend Shuttlesworth's words, for "human supremacy."

5

THE MARCH ON WASHINGTON

AFTER the Freedom Rides of 1961, the tide of black nonviolent protest rose rapidly, and by 1963 civil rights had become America's hottest political issue. Some 1,200 people had ridden desegregated buses into the segregated South in the summer of 1961; two years later, 100,000 people demonstrated against racism in Birmingham and other southern cities. The protests resulted in nearly 15,000 arrests across the South. President Kennedy realized that unless Congress enacted a sweeping civil rights bill, racial unrest would probably spread, pushing violence to new highs.

Kennedy's advisers warned him that many southern whites thought he had already shown too much sympathy for Martin Luther King, Jr. Further civil rights action, said the aides, might cost Kennedy the 1964 election. But Robert Kennedy urged his brother to move ahead with vigor. The president agreed, saying, "There comes a time when a man has to take a stand and history will record that he has to meet these tough situations" and, no matter the cost, "make a decision."

Martin Luther King, Jr. (front row, fourth from left), joins hands with other civil rights leaders during the 1963 March on Washington. Gathered under a cloudless blue sky, more than a quarter of a million Americans later heard King say, "I have a dream . . ."

Surrounded by Alabama highway patrolmen, Governor George Wallace confronts U.S. Justice Department officials at the University of Alabama. The June 1963 standoff sprang from Wallace's refusal to admit two black students to the all-white college.

Kennedy took his stand on June 11, 1963, shortly after Alabama governor George Corley Wallace personally blocked the path of two black students trying to register at the University of Alabama. Earlier, on being sworn in as governor, Wallace had sneered at civil rights leaders: "I draw the line in the dust," he said, "and I say, Segregation now! Segregation tomor-

row! Segregation forever!" Now, determined to carry out that pledge, Wallace stood in front of the college admissions office until federal marshals, sent by Robert Kennedy, ordered him to let the students pass.

The governor's gesture of defiance appealed to some white voters in Alabama, but the image he projected on national television was almost as shocking and offensive as that of Bull Connor's dogs attacking peaceful marchers. To Americans trying to forget the horrors of Birmingham, the sight of a governor physically seeking to stop two qualified students from entering a school because of their color was at once embarrassing and tragic. To John Kennedy it was the moment to warn the Wallaces and Connors of the land that their day was over.

In the evening after Wallace's stand, the president spoke on national television about "a moral issue" that was "as old as the Scriptures" and "as clear as the American Constitution." The crisis arising from racial discrimination could not be "met by repressive police action," he said, but only by prompt efforts to see that "all Americans are to be afforded equal rights and equal opportunities." Toward that end he would ask Congress "to make a commitment it has not fully made in this century" to the belief "that race has no place in American life or law."

Martin Luther King, Jr., hailed Kennedy's speech as "the most earnest, human, and profound appeal for understanding and justice that any president has uttered since the first days of the Republic." On June 19, the president followed with a request to Congress for a sweeping civil rights measure to protect voting rights, ban segregation in public places, and deny government funds for programs that excluded or segregated blacks. The outlook for Kennedy's bill was uncertain, and his standing among southern whites dropped sharply. But there could be no turning back. The president had fully committed the authority of his office—and his political future—to continued civil rights progress.

As Congress slowly pondered and debated Kennedy's specific proposals, black leaders searched for a way to build support for his Civil Rights Bill. In July 1963, 73-year-old black labor leader A. Philip Randolph came up with such a way: he announced plans for a rally in the nation's capital to demand federal protection of black rights. To show that this demand was a matter not of color but of justice, he invited whites as well as blacks to participate.

Randolph's event had been a long time coming. In 1941 he had first proposed a march on Washington to protest the defense industry's refusal to hire blacks. When President Franklin Roosevelt formed a committee to promote fair hiring practices, Randolph canceled the march, to the bitter disappointment of some younger blacks. In 1963, with the black revolution giving new muscle to Randolph's decades-old vision, the aging labor leader once more hoped that a march on Washington could impress on the nation the moral and political power of the civil rights cause.

The task of fulfilling Randolph's dream fell to his close aide Bayard Rustin, at 51 the most skillful organizer in the civil rights movement. Tall, with flaring gray hair, high cheekbones, and an accent that reflected long stays in England, Rustin appeared a model of elegance. As a young man in the 1930s he had sung in all-white clubs with such black celebrities as Josh White and Leadbelly; later he turned to working full time on reform causes.

Rustin, a pioneer in nonviolent protest during the 1940s, had spent a year in India studying with disciples of Mohandas Gandhi. A Hindu leader whose nonviolent resistance to British colonial rule hastened India's progress toward independence, Gandhi had later inspired such reformers as Martin Luther King, Jr., and James Farmer. In 1963 the challenge of coordinating a massive rally in the nation's capital marked Rustin's stiffest test in combining his faith in nonviolence with his devotion to the movement for black rights.

Privately, civil rights leaders disagreed sharply over the plans for a march on Washington, but they repeatedly compromised their differences to promote a common cause. Randolph himself was the first to alter his vision of the march in hopes of broadening his base of support. As a veteran labor organizer, he had originally planned a rally to demand a federal jobs program for the poor and unemployed. But he soon realized that blacks in the South cared far more about protesting segregation, and so he began to emphasize passage of the Civil Rights Bill. This shift gained an endorsement of the march from Martin Luther King, Jr., and with it the chance to mobilize the black masses.

Other civil rights leaders similarly swallowed their reservations. James Farmer of CORE and John Lewis of SNCC doubted that a march would make for a strong enough protest, but when King backed Randolph, they supported him as well. Roy Wilkins of the more conservative NAACP feared that the march might do more harm than good; if it appeared too disruptive, he said, it could provoke a backlash by Congress, the president, and the American people. But King reassured Wilkins that there would be no sit-ins, boycotts, or other such actions at the Capitol. As religious, labor, and other groups stepped forward to help sponsor the march, the tone of the event became milder still, abandoning any hint of protest against the government.

The march leaders tried to expand their common ground with the president at a White House conference on June 22, 1963. Kennedy expressed appreciation for their support of his Civil Rights Bill, but cautioned that further demonstrations might anger Americans and hurt the chances of passage. "We want success in Congress," he said, "not just a big show at the Capitol."

Kennedy's guests explained that the black masses were already angry over the failure to protect their rights, and were going to vent their frustrations regardless of what their leaders said. The march would at least give a nonviolent outlet for their rising impa-

tience. Martin Luther King, Jr., added that he had never engaged in a campaign for change that did not seem "ill-timed" to some people.

The White House conference produced an informal agreement. Randolph and his fellow civil rights leaders persuaded Kennedy to endorse the aims of the rally; he, in turn, further discouraged them from considering any protest against his administration. At the close of the meeting, Kennedy said that they might at times disagree over tactics, but they should always preserve "confidence in the good faith of each other."

As the march date approached, even the speeches written for the event were monitored and in one instance muzzled for the sake of unity. John Lewis, the young chairman of SNCC who had braved numerous

Labor leader A. Philip Randolph (left) and his aide, activist Bayard Rustin, answer questions at a Washington press conference. The 1963 March on Washington, the largest political rally the United States had ever known, owed much of its success to these two civil rights pioneers.

it was not so much the fiery tone of Lewis's text that bothered him; it was the fact that Lewis was denouncing the nation's political system at a rally "called in large part to back the Civil Rights Bill—and that seemed like a doublecross."

Lewis was not a man to back down easily, whether the challenge came from racists or fellow civil rights reformers. But Randolph, the white-haired sage of the movement, revered by all parties, spoke to Lewis for the others. "We've come this far," he implored. "For the sake of unity, change it." Lewis reluctantly did so, and the March on Washington went forward with ranks closed for the sake of moving a nation.

On August 28, 1963, under a nearly cloudless sky, more than a quarter of a million people gathered near the Lincoln Memorial for the largest single protest demonstration in U.S. history. Fifty thousand whites mingled in the crowd and among the prominent speakers. From every area of American life people came to donate their talents or simply their prestige to the cause of "jobs and freedom."

Present at the rally were film stars Sidney Poitier, Charlton Heston, and Marlon Brando; radical folksinger Joan Baez and gospel legend Mahalia Jackson; teachers, students, professionals; clergymen of every faith. And although many Washington residents had anticipated the event in terror (a black presidential adviser later observed that the army had prepared for the rally "as if it were World War II"), the immense crowd was nonviolent and in a largely festive mood.

The sweltering afternoon featured many speakers, each given 15 minutes, though more than a few found that their wisdom could not be contained in that brief time. The dominant memory of the rally, however, was the closing address by Martin Luther King, Jr. He began with a formal description of the trials of African Americans struggling for freedom from the shackles of racial discrimination.

King was gathering up his notes and preparing to sit down when Mahalia Jackson called out from behind him, "Tell them about your dream, Martin! Tell them about the dream!" King obliged, drawing on images from earlier speeches, encouragement from the assembled marchers, and sheer inspiration. To shouts

King approaches the end of his prepared speech on the day of the march. No one present would ever forget what followed.

of "Tell it, doctor!" and "Amen!" the minister put aside his text and concluded:

> I have a dream that one day this nation will rise up and live out the true meaning of its creed: "We hold these truths to be self-evident—that all men are created equal." I have a dream that one day on the red hills of Georgia the sons of former slaves and the sons of former slave owners will be able to sit down together at the table of brother-hood. . . . I have a dream that my four little children will one day live in a nation where they will not be judged by the color of their skin but by the content of their character. I have a dream today! . . .
>
> When we allow freedom to ring, when we let it ring from every village and every hamlet, from every state and every city, we will be able to speed up that day when all of God's children—black men and white men, Jews and Gentiles, Protestants and Catholics—will be able to join hands and sing in the words of the old Negro spiritual, "Free at last! Free at last! Thank God almighty, we are free at last!"

Weary with emotion, King stepped down from the podium and into the embrace of his friend and fellow minister Ralph Abernathy. The Holy Spirit, exclaimed Abernathy, had surely taken hold of King as he spoke. And in the faces of a quarter-million black and white listeners, now suddenly re-leased in shouts of praise, King could glimpse his ideal of interracial brotherhood come to thundering, joyful life.

The black novelist James Baldwin, who had often written in critical, disbelieving tones about King's politics of faith, was among the cheering multitudes. Later he confessed to feeling the irresistible power of the minister's vision of racial harmony: "That day, for a moment, it almost seemed that we stood on a height . . . perhaps we could make the kingdom real, perhaps the beloved community would not forever remain that dream one dreamed in agony."

The vision seemed closer still because of the march's impact on President Kennedy. Up until the march date he had been concerned over possible violence that could discredit the event and his own leadership for civil rights. Afterward, though, a relieved president invited 10 of the main organizers, including John Lewis, to a reception in the White House, offering them warm encouragement and hot coffee. Kennedy also publicly praised "the deep fervor and the quiet dignity that characterizes the thousands who have gathered in the nation's capital from across the country to demonstrate their faith and confidence in our democratic form of government."

Just before the triumphant March on Washington, a triumphant life—that of one of America's greatest black leaders and intellects—had come to an end. William Edward Burghardt Du Bois (universally known as W. E. B. Du Bois), a founder of the NAACP and longtime editor of its influential publication, *The Crisis*, made an indelible mark on American culture by his work as an author, editor, and educator. Born in Massachusetts in 1868, Du Bois received his education at Fisk University, Harvard, and the University of Berlin (Germany). He passionately advocated the elimination of discrimination against black Americans; although professing love for his native land, Du Bois spent most of his life criticizing the American social order and its methodical suppression of blacks. In 1961 he exiled himself to the African nation of Ghana, where he died on August 17, 1963, at the age of 95.

Great challenges still faced the movement. The March on Washington had powerfully conveyed the serious and responsible intent of civil rights support-

Summoned by President John F. Kennedy (fourth from right), civil rights leaders assemble at the White House after the March on Washington. Next to the president are labor leader A. Philip Randolph (left) and Vice-President Lyndon B. Johnson. Other guests include Whitney Young of the National Urban League (third from left), Martin Luther King, Jr. (right of Young), SNCC's John Lewis (right of King), and Roy Wilkins of the NAACP (far right).

ers, but it changed few votes in Congress. Meanwhile, southern congressmen were vowing an all-out effort to defeat Kennedy's civil rights measure. More alarming still was a rise in extremist violence. The following September a dynamite blast rocked Birmingham's famous Sixteenth Street Baptist Church and killed four black girls who were attending Sunday school. No city official cared—or dared—to attend the funeral service for the victims.

The president spoke out strongly against the unreasoning acts of violence, but increasingly he found himself a target of hatred because of his support for civil rights. Kennedy was nonetheless determined to ride out the fury of the South's white conservatives and to encourage the region's white moderates. By late fall of 1963 signs of progress were appearing. Many southern communities had desegregated at least some public facilities. In Congress Kennedy's Civil Rights Bill took a major step forward: on October 29, a key committee in the House of Representatives favorably reported the bill by a comfortable margin.

At a November 1963 press conference, called just before he left for a Dallas, Texas, political visit, Kennedy predicted that before Congress adjourned it would pass his Civil Rights Bill. He believed that the future had never looked brighter, and civil rights leaders agreed.

NOW

STUDENT NONVIOLENT COORDINATING COMMITTEE
8½ RAYMOND STREET, N.W. ATLANTA 14, GEORGIA

6

FREEDOM SUMMER

A S Martin Luther King, Jr., and his family sat by
their television set on November 22, 1963,
they heard the shocking news from Dallas: a sniper
had shot and mortally wounded the president of the
United States. Coretta King remembered the family's
pain that day: "We felt that President Kennedy had
been a friend of the Cause and that with him as
president we could continue to move forward. We
watched and prayed for him. Then it was announced
that the president was dead. Martin had been very
quiet during this period. Finally he said, 'This is what
is going to happen to me also.'"

Black Americans sharing the national tragedy
over Kennedy's murder felt a special, added concern.
Without Kennedy to oppose the rising tide of racial
hatred, would Congress dare pass the strong civil
rights measures he had asked for? No one questioned
the political skills of the new president of the United
States, Lyndon B. Johnson. Yet this native Texan had
been raised on Jim Crow traditions, and he was known
for having blocked or weakened civil rights legislation
during his years in Congress. In the gloom of November 1963, blacks asked whether Johnson could ever be
a true friend to their cause.

*The Student Nonviolent Coordinating Committee, whose bold
spirit is captured in this poster, directed its efforts in the early
1960s to organizing African Americans in Mississippi, the
South's poorest and most conservative state.*

After signing the Civil Rights Act of 1964 with a handful of symbolic pens, President Lyndon Johnson gives King a handshake and one of the pens. Later that day, the president would give him something else: the suggestion that, because the new law "secured the rights Negroes possessed," future civil rights actions might be "unnecessary and possibly even self-defeating."

But Johnson's critics underestimated his ability to adapt. In the fast-moving 1960s, he saw that civil rights had become an issue of great political importance; furthermore, he felt personally touched by the demonstrations against segregation. Within days of Kennedy's assassination, Johnson demanded that Congress pass Kennedy's Civil Rights Bill with no changes at all. He was determined to show that a southerner could be as firm a champion of freedom as any other American.

In the first month of his new presidency, Johnson bestowed the nation's highest civilian peacetime honor, the Presidential Medal of Freedom, on two African Americans. Legendary contralto Marian Anderson and tireless international peacemaker Ralph Bunche received the coveted medals at the White House on December 7, 1963. Bunche, said the president, had made "outstanding contributions to the ideals of peace and democracy"; Anderson had "ennobled her race and her country, while her voice . . . enthralled the world."

Back on the political front, Johnson had set himself the greatest challenge of his career. The Civil Rights Bill was a measure of breathtaking scope, with clauses to end racial discrimination in public facilities, voting, and hiring. The bill would also cut off federal funds to segregated institutions, including schools. Many southern whites, who considered segregation natural and right, saw this bill as a threat to their way of life, and their representatives in Congress vowed bitter, all-out resistance.

Among the hundreds of men and women lobbying for passage of the Civil Rights Bill, none was more forceful than the NAACP's Clarence Mitchell. A black man in a white man's world (in the early 1960s, there were no blacks in the Senate and only five blacks in the House), Mitchell had nevertheless so impressed Washington's power circles that he was sometimes called "the 101st senator." Possessing apparently unlimited energy, Mitchell also had unswerving faith in his ability to persuade congressmen that commitment to racial justice was a key test of American democracy. Assistant Attorney General Nicholas B. Katzenbach commented admiringly on Mitchell's perseverance. He would visit each congressman's office and, said Katzenbach, if he "wasn't thrown out bodily he'd mark it down as favorable." In the early months of 1964, Mitchell's whirlwind efforts did much to rally lawmakers to the side of black rights.

On February 10, 1964, the House of Representatives passed the Civil Rights Bill by the decisive vote of 290 to 130. After more than four months of bitter political infighting, the Senate followed suit, and the Civil Rights Act of 1964, every major feature intact, emerged for presidential signature. Johnson signed it into law on July 2, 1964.

During the drive to pass the momentous legislation, the young men and women of the Student Nonviolent Coordinating Committee had been hard at work on their own project—one well suited to their taste for daring action. Their aim was to organize African Americans politically in Mississippi, a state whose earth was deeply stained with the blood of murdered blacks.

Mississippi had always drawn emphatic racial lines, harsh even for the Deep South. A late-blooming slave state, it had forced blacks into labor gangs with a ruthlessness unknown in older southern states such as Virginia. Until the mid-20th century, the civil rights movement had barely challenged Mississippi's caste system. Senator James Eastland and other rich white planters still controlled vast cotton tracts on which black sharecroppers labored from sunrise to sunset for perhaps 50 cents a day. Elsewhere in the South, blacks stirred with news of the successful bus boycott in Montgomery; in Mississippi, white supremacy and black terror continued to define race relations.

The South's most conservative state was also its poorest—and its most violent. Following the Supreme Court's 1954 *Brown v. Board of Education* desegregation decision, a wave of racial assaults lashed Mississippi. The horror climaxed in the August 1955 lynching of 14-year-old Emmett Till, a Chicago-born youth who was visiting relatives in Money, Mississippi. For greeting a white woman in a candy store (he said, "Bye, baby," as he left the shop), the youth was dragged from his relatives' home by three white men who beat him savagely, then shot him dead. The men

mutilated the boy's body and threw it into the Talla-hatchie River.

Identified by witnesses, two of the men were arrested and tried for murder. In a widely reported trial, the defense lawyer appealed to the white racial identity of the 12 jurors, and although the prosecution delivered clear evidence of the men's guilt, the jury acquitted them of all charges. The U.S. attorney then charged them with kidnapping (a federal crime, and therefore under federal, not state, jurisdiction), but a grand jury—made up of white Mississippians—refused to indict them, and the government was forced to abandon the case.

Mamie Bradley grieves as the body of her son, 14-year-old Emmett Till, arrives at a Chicago railroad station. For the crime of speaking to a white woman, Emmett had been brutally killed by three white men in Money, Mississippi.

Roy Bryant (left) and his half brother J. W. Milam (center) await trial for Emmet Till's murder. Despite strong evidence of the pair's guilt, an all-white jury acquitted them.

Black Mississippians who dared ask for political rights sharply increased their chances of encountering white violence. In 1955, just before national attention focused on the Emmett Till case, a black man who had recently voted in the state's Democratic primary was shot dead at high noon on the courthouse steps in Brookhaven, Mississippi. State NAACP director Medgar Evers, meanwhile, spent his days recruiting members and his nights sleeping beside his rifle. It had been Evers who helped James Meredith break the ancient color line at "Ole Miss"—the University of Mississippi—in 1962.

On June 12, 1963—the night that John F. Kennedy asked the nation to support a strong civil rights law—the 37-year-old Evers attended a civil rights rally at a church near his Jackson, Mississippi, home. As he left his car, a sniper fired at him from ambush: Evers died instantly. Byron de la Beckwith, a White Citizens' Council member, stood trial for the murder, but legal complications led to years of irresolution; finally, in February 1994, de la Beckwith was found guilty.

Led by Bob Moses, a shy, 26-year-old, Harlem-born, Harvard-educated high school teacher, SNCC workers first entered the unpromising state of Mississippi in 1961. When he had joined SNCC as a volunteer, Moses had noted that most civil rights groups based their southern headquarters in the comfortable, relatively tolerant capital city of Atlanta, and that most looked for new members in urban areas. But SNCC, Moses told his fellow members, could help the movement even more by working with rural blacks in areas of greater danger.

Mississippi NAACP director Medgar Evers checks mail in his Jackson office. On June 12, 1963—one year after he helped James Meredith break the color barrier at the University of Mississippi—Evers fell to an assassin's bullet, a crime unpunished for 30 years.

Robert Moses tells reporters he will send civil rights workers into the countryside. The young SNCC leader invited students of all races to help him organize black voters in southwest Mississippi.

His idea won approval, and with a small staff, Moses went into the wilderness of McComb, Mississippi.

Shortly after Moses arrived in McComb, a state legislator warned a black resident not to register to vote. The man registered anyway, and the legislator shot him dead in broad daylight. A jury conceded that the official had done the shooting, but acquitted him nonetheless. By late 1961, a stream of such violent acts had made it nearly impossible for SNCC to recruit new voters in Mississippi. Then the Kennedy administration offered unexpected aid.

Attorney General Robert Kennedy promised that if all the civil rights groups concerned with southern black voting rights—SNCC, CORE, SCLC, and the NAACP—joined hands in an intensive southern voter registration effort, he would arrange to have the effort funded by liberal-minded foundations. In early 1962, SNCC joined with the other organizations in launching the Voter Education Project (VEP), whose founding charter quoted John Kennedy's inaugural address on the need to defend liberty at any cost.

By 1964, VEP had registered over half a million southern blacks, but its record in Mississippi was dismal. To the deep disappointment of SNCC activists, in two years they had added fewer than 4,000 names to the Mississippi voting rolls and left some 394,000 black adults unregistered. Mississippi police frequently arrested SNCC workers and joined with private citizens in harassing and beating them. Sometimes angry whites went further. In February 1963 Moses and two other organizers were riding a dark road in Greenwood when thirteen 45-caliber bullets tore through the car, shattering the left window and wounding the driver in the neck. The incident reminded SNCC workers yet again that in Mississippi they had about the same legal protection as outlaws.

Nevertheless, SNCC youths continued to pour into Mississippi. Joining them in 1963 were 80 Stanford and Yale university students, most of them white, who helped Mississippi's blacks act on their political concerns. In dozens of cities and towns, some 80,000 blacks voted for "Freedom party" delegate slates in alternate elections to the state's all-white Democratic primaries. The votes were never tallied by the party's Jim Crow electoral boards, but they showed that Mississippi's blacks did care about the ballot, despite repeated claims by whites to the contrary. The outpouring of black voters also led Bob Moses to wonder what a much larger organizing effort in Mississippi could achieve.

Moses planned a 1964 "Freedom Summer" project in which hundreds of student volunteers would move into every black neighborhood in Mississippi to encourage registration and support for candidates of the Freedom party. Some black activists already in Mississippi, however, were not pleased. They argued that the presence of an interracial team would simply anger authorities and harm efforts to gain the confidence of local blacks. They feared, too, that educated northern white students would take over leadership roles, pushing aside local blacks.

But Bob Moses refused to be part of an all-black project. Integration, he explained, was at the heart of the Beloved Community ideal, which had inspired him and others to nonviolent sacrifice. His stand helped ensure that the Freedom Summer would continue SNCC's interracial traditions.

Moses and the other planners of the Freedom Summer project had another, less widely talked-about reason to welcome white volunteers. They believed that only if whites shared the risks of violence would civil rights workers gain a national hearing and federal protection. David Dennis of CORE later explained that if volunteers were going to be murdered, the "death of a white college student would bring on more attention to what was going on than for a black college student getting it." That, added Dennis, was "cold," but it was "also in another sense speaking the language of the country."

Applications from young volunteers soon flooded the planning offices. Typically, they were Ivy League students, comfortable enough to give up a summer's employment and pay their way south, and idealistic enough to give up a pleasant suburban life in order to work for social change.

Mississippi prepared for the arrival of civil rights workers as if threatened by a foreign army. Governor Paul Johnson increased the number of state highway patrolmen from 275 to 475. In Jackson, the state capital, the police force nearly doubled. Mayor Allen Thompson bought 250 shotguns and had them loaded with buckshot and mounted on squad cars and motorcycles. The mayor also readied his "Thompson tank," a six-ton armored vehicle with thick steel walls, bulletproof windows, and a submachine gun on the turret.

In mid-June the student volunteers set out for Oxford, Ohio, to begin their training for the Freedom Summer. Although all had read about racial violence in the South, many students were shocked by the stories they heard from the black activists who tried to prepare them emotionally for the dangers ahead.

R. Jess Brown, one of four lawyers in the state of Mississippi who would accept civil rights workers as clients, explained to his young audience that where they were going, they would have no rights worth mentioning: "If you're riding down somewhere and a cop stops you and starts to put you under arrest even though you haven't committed any crime," he said, "go on to jail." Another speaker told these future civil rights workers: "There's not even a sharp line between living and dying; it is just a thin fuzz."

Perhaps the single greatest shock at the training camp came when a Justice Department spokesman warned that the FBI could investigate acts of violence but it could not actually protect the students. A spectacled black man in overalls screamed at him, "What are you going to do to enable us to see the fall?" "Nothing," the official replied, and added, "The responsibility for protection is that of the local police." Students shouted in protest at this seeming lack of concern for their lives. In the privacy of their rooms, many cried. Black attorney Len Holt thought the training sessions were successful: when the students arrived in Oxford, he observed, they "were merely scared," but by the time they packed their belongings for the trip to Mississippi, "they were terrified."

On June 21, as carloads of volunteers arrived in Mississippi, they learned that a black church in the town of Philadelphia had just been set on fire. Three volunteers, Michael Schwerner, James Chaney, and Andrew Goodman, immediately set out for Philadelphia to reassure local blacks. Schwerner, a 24-year-old social worker from New York, was among the few whites who had spent time in Mississippi, working with his wife, Rita, to help blacks in the town of Meridian build a community house.

Chaney, a 19-year-old black native of Meridian, joined Schwerner early on, despite his mother's concern: "Ain't you afraid of this?" she had asked. "Naw, mama," replied Chaney, "that's what's the matter now—everybody's scared." Now Chaney rode with Schwerner to Philadelphia in order to quiet those fears in others.

The third rider, 20-year-old Andrew Goodman, came from a background more typical of the volunteers: he was a student at Queens College in New York City who had never set foot in Mississippi. But Goodman's courage made him a welcome passenger on the lonely trip.

Under the baleful glares of angry white onlookers, the three young men traveled through 35 miles of road lined with swamp, scrub pine, and scraggly cotton land. They were never heard from again. By late afternoon on June 21, volunteers began to ask around but learned nothing. By the next morning, veterans of the movement had assumed the worst: that

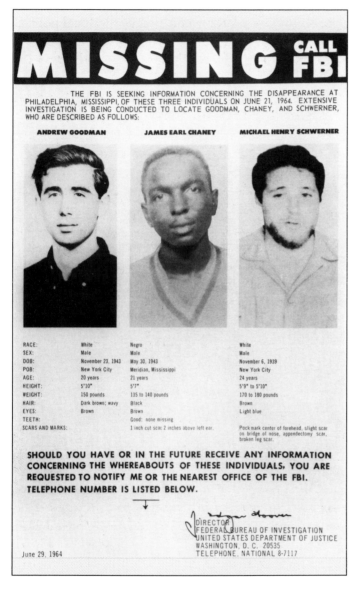

MISSING CALL FBI

THE FBI IS SEEKING INFORMATION CONCERNING THE DISAPPEARANCE AT PHILADELPHIA, MISSISSIPPI, OF THESE THREE INDIVIDUALS ON JUNE 21, 1964. EXTENSIVE INVESTIGATION IS BEING CONDUCTED TO LOCATE GOODMAN, CHANEY, AND SCHWERNER, WHO ARE DESCRIBED AS FOLLOWS:

ANDREW GOODMAN   **JAMES EARL CHANEY**   **MICHAEL HENRY SCHWERNER**

RACE:	White	Negro	White
SEX:	Male	Male	Male
DOB:	November 23, 1943	May 30, 1943	November 6, 1939
POB:	New York City	Meridian, Mississippi	New York City
AGE:	20 years	21 years	24 years
HEIGHT:	5'10"	5'7"	5'9" to 5'10"
WEIGHT:	150 pounds	135 to 140 pounds	170 to 180 pounds
HAIR:	Dark brown; wavy	Black	Brown
EYES:	Brown	Brown	Light blue
TEETH:		Good: none missing	
SCARS AND MARKS:		1 inch cut scar 2 inches above left ear.	Pock mark center of forehead, slight scar on bridge of nose, appendectomy scar, broken leg scar.

SHOULD YOU HAVE OR IN THE FUTURE RECEIVE ANY INFORMATION CONCERNING THE WHEREABOUTS OF THESE INDIVIDUALS, YOU ARE REQUESTED TO NOTIFY ME OR THE NEAREST OFFICE OF THE FBI. TELEPHONE NUMBER IS LISTED BELOW.

DIRECTOR
FEDERAL BUREAU OF INVESTIGATION
UNITED STATES DEPARTMENT OF JUSTICE
WASHINGTON, D. C. 20535
TELEPHONE, NATIONAL 8-7117

June 29, 1964

An FBI poster asks for information about Andrew Goodman, James Earl Chaney, and Michael Schwerner, young civil rights workers who disappeared on their way to investigate a firebombing in Philadelphia, Mississippi. In August 1964, six weeks after their disappearance, the FBI found them—shot to death and buried in an earthen dam near Philadelphia.

Schwerner, Chaney, and Goodman had become the first victims of the Freedom Summer.

Fear and gloom swept through the camps of volunteers waiting for word of their missing colleagues. A young woman wrote to her parents that the news was almost unbelievable: "They were in Oxford only a few days before—they couldn't be in such danger."

Mississippi youths take classes at a Freedom School, one of the many informal academies at which SNCC volunteers taught black children in the 1960s. Subjects included foreign languages, math, art, and other subjects not offered to black students by the state's public schools.

But suddenly she was hit with a chilling thought: "It could be you. And then there's this weird feeling of guilt because it wasn't you."

Weighed down by a sense of constant danger and lack of support by the federal government, the volunteers threw themselves into the work of organizing local blacks. But this, too, had its discouraging side. Many volunteers had expected a rush of eager black sharecroppers to the nearest registration office, but it did not work out that way. Black Mississippians greeted their visitors politely but often remained unwilling to disobey the local authorities by registering to vote. They knew that any political act might cost them their jobs, their homes, even their lives.

But the volunteers persisted and, in time, blacks began coming to registration classes. In McComb, where more acts of racial violence occurred than in any other town in Mississippi, a volunteer saw the black community's growing determination: "The voter registration classes are slightly tense, but what is more present is hope. . . . The people dress up carefully. They shake each other's hands, await eagerly the return of those who have gone down to the courthouse already." Many had great trouble reading and filling out the forms. "But they're going down."

The heart of this political awakening did not depend on white registrars at all. In late July local blacks chaired meetings of an independent organization, the Mississippi Freedom Democratic party, created as an alternative to the state's official, whites-only Democratic party. Volunteers remarked in amazement and pride at the way people who had been politically silent their whole lives now needed all of 10 minutes before speaking up on issues of taxes, fairness, and rights with the confidence of longtime activists.

For many volunteers the most important work did not involve political organizing but rather the creation of "Freedom Schools" for the children of local blacks. These schools provided special help in reading, as well as classes on African American history, race relations, and other subjects no Mississippi public school would dare permit black children even to hear about, let alone speak about.

Among the classes students asked for most often in the Freedom Schools were foreign languages, arithmetic, art, drama, typing, and journalism—none of which was available to them in the public schools. Suddenly free to learn in any area, students carried out bold new projects: in Holly Springs, a student-produced play, *Seeds of Freedom*, about the slain NAACP leader Medgar Evers; in Clarksdale, a "freedom press," typed and edited by the students; in Hattiesburg, the center of the Freedom School movement, a student-written declaration of independence seeking racial equality in Mississippi.

All these efforts occurred in an atmosphere of constant terror. White Mississippians harassed the young volunteers daily with arrests, threatening phone calls, and spying by the Ku Klux Klan. In Drew, police jailed volunteers for giving out voter registration material; in Hattiesburg, workers were beaten; in McComb, a Freedom House was bombed.

A volunteer who had witnessed many violent incidents and suffered a beating in broad daylight wrote to his family, "I wake up in the morning sighing with relief that I was not bombed, because I know that 'they' know where I live. And I think, well, I got through that night, now I have to get through this day, and it goes on and on." While this volunteer wrote his letter, a phone caller threatened to bomb the office.

Meanwhile, in response to a growing public outcry, President Johnson turned up the FBI's hunt for Schwerner, Chaney, and Goodman. In early August the search ended at an earthen dam in Philadelphia, Mississippi, where the bodies of the three civil rights workers were uncovered. All had been shot; Chaney, the lone black, had also been viciously beaten. Evidence soon pointed to Philadelphia's deputy sheriff, who had arranged for the three youths to be "released" from jail just long enough for several whites to catch and murder them.

News reporters found Michael Schwerner's widow, Rita, and asked about her feelings. She offered a brief word on the nation's loss: "Three good men were killed—three good men who could have done a great deal for their country." The reporters pressed her to state whether some good might yet come from the triple murder. Her reply captured the hopes and doubts of all the volunteers: "That is up to the people of the United States."

7

FROM SELMA
TO MONTGOMERY

Black activists continued to prod and inspire Congress with nonviolent protests against Jim Crow. In the summer of 1965, their actions centered on Selma, Alabama, a city in which blacks made up a majority of the 29,000 inhabitants but only 3 percent of the voting rolls. Situated on a height overlooking the muddy Alabama River, Selma had been a major market for cotton and slaves before the Civil War. One hundred years later, mule-drawn, cotton-laden wagons still lumbered down Selma's streets. And still standing among the town's stately buildings was a three-story house where as many as 500 slaves were once auctioned off on a brisk business day.

Selma was known as a center of southern white resistance to the civil rights movement. It was here that Montgomery's Bull Connor had been born, here that Alabama's intensely racist White Citizens' Council first met. In late 1962, a SNCC worker had scouted the city, hoping to find a black community ready to demand its rights. Glumly returning to SNCC's Atlanta headquarters, he went to the community-organizing map and crossed out Selma.

Guarding the entrance of the courthouse, "Big Jim" Clark, sheriff of Dallas County, Alabama, demonstrates his system for dealing with black would-be voters. It involved barking out individuals' voter-registration numbers in rapid succession, and turning back all those who failed to respond instantly.

Shortly after the volunteer's disheartening gesture, Bernard Lafayette, a SNCC worker and former member of the Nashville student protests, found himself between projects. He picked Selma as a welcome challenge. Early in 1963 he and several other SNCC members spent several months there, visiting black homes to discuss the way officials had limited the number of registered black voters in the county.

Lafayette explained to black residents that the voter registration board met only two days a month and rejected black applicants who failed simply to cross a "t" in registration forms. If an applicant managed to hand in a letter-perfect form, registrars would ask him or her "basic" questions about constitutional rights ("What two rights does a person have after being charged by a grand jury?") that would have stumped most professors. Some time later the black would-be voter would receive a brief letter saying he or she had failed the tests, with no further explanation. But by that point, the applicant needed no explanation: it was clear that to the white registrars, one constitutional right a dark-skinned American did not have was the right to vote.

Selma's blacks welcomed the SNCC workers and began going with them in small numbers to the downtown courthouse to protest the treatment of black applicants. Then came weekly mass meetings to explain how the ballot could help overcome the daily humiliations that blacks suffered in Selma. Those humiliations worsened as blacks tried to register to vote. Thirty-two teachers lost their jobs for daring to show up at the courthouse. John Lewis went to jail for leading a picket line at the forbidden building. SNCC leader Jim Forman spoke to a voter-registration meeting at the Tabernacle Baptist Church, then waited with his audience until a posse of several hundred whites armed with clubs and cattle prods grew tired of staking out the area.

That posse belonged to Big Jim Clark, one of the toughest sheriffs in the southern Black Belt, a crescent-shaped area of rich black soil that stretches from the Alabama River to northeast Mississippi. The Black Belt was home to a large population of African Americans, most of whom boasted no wealth, no power, and no rights. Hoping to find safety in numbers, SNCC workers joined with several hundred of these local blacks on October 7, 1963, for a "Freedom Day" march to the county courthouse. But Clark showed up, too.

A towering presence draped in gold braid, the sheriff sported a lapel button that answered black hopes in one word: "NEVER." As a crowd of grinning whites shouted, "Get 'em, Big Jim! Get 'em!" Clark began arresting the SNCC workers on the courthouse steps. His men fanned out to keep others from bringing food and water to the 350 blacks waiting outside the courthouse to register.

Thwarted this time by Clark's physical force, Selma's blacks decided to get some "soul force": to attend their next voter registration drive, they invited none other than Martin Luther King, Jr. The civil rights leader had recently returned from Oslo, Norway, where he became the youngest person and the second black in history to be awarded the Nobel Peace Prize. (Black American diplomat Ralph Bunche had won it in 1950.)

At the Nobel award ceremony, King said he accepted the prize on behalf of the whole American civil rights movement, of which he regarded himself only as a trustee. He hoped to share, he told the international audience, his "abiding faith in America and audacious faith in the future of mankind." Asked by reporters why he thought he had won the Peace Prize, King said it was to recognize the fact that "nonviolence is the answer to the crucial political and moral question of our time—the need for men to overcome oppression and violence without resorting to violence and oppression."

Even before leaving for Oslo, King had been thinking about launching a voter registration drive throughout Alabama; Selma seemed as good a place to start as any. Not only had SNCC helped organize the town's black residents, but the hot-tempered Sheriff Clark might do even more than Bull Connor, King believed, to draw the nation's attention to racist outrages.

Arriving in Selma on January 14, 1965, King agreed to join the march scheduled for the following day. When the marchers arrived at the courthouse, however, they once again found their way blocked by Jim Clark. He waved one of the black activists, Amelia Boynton, aside because her pace displeased him. Seizing the tall, stout woman by her collar, Clark shoved her halfway down the block and into a waiting police car. Then he ordered the arrest—on grounds of "unlawful assembly"—of 67 of the blacks seeking to register.

Selma's mayor, Joseph Smitherman, watched Clark's antics in dismay. Speaking in an almost apologetic tone, he told reporters that the sheriff was "out of control." The newsmen scribbled furiously, recording Clark's every astonishing move for the American public. But Clark was only just hitting his stride. On Friday, January 22, 105 black teachers—representing one of the most conservative groups in the black community—put on their best Sabbath-day clothes and marched slowly around the courthouse in silent protest. Clark and his deputies chased them away with clubs and electric cattle prods.

Three days later, blacks marched to the courthouse under protection of a federal court order: city and county officials were now forbidden to block the "orderly process" of voter registration. Clark did not care. He swaggered up and down the line, bullying people with threats and shoves. When 53-year-old Annie Lee Cooper defiantly told Clark, "There ain't nobody scared around here," Clark pushed her off balance. But Cooper, at 225 pounds, was even larger than Clark, and now she was also angrier. A single punch dropped Clark to his knees, and a second sent him to the ground. One of Clark's deputies grabbed the woman from behind, but she stepped on his foot and elbowed him in the stomach, freeing herself long enough to knock Clark down once more.

At last three deputies pinned Cooper to the ground, and Clark faced a moment of truth. Reporters were looking on, ready to record and photograph any improper move. "I wish you would hit me, you scum," sneered Cooper. Without hesitation, he slammed his billy club down on her head, the sound of the blow traveling to the edge of the watching crowd. Clark then sat astride Cooper's body and clubbed her senseless. Reporters wrote frantically; television cameras rolled; news photographers snapped and flashed. The next day, almost every TV station and newspaper in the country showed the image of law and order, Sheriff Clark style.

By late February, as pressure built in the Congress for a law to strengthen black voting rights, the tensions in Selma spilled over into nearby towns. In the rural community of Marion, state troopers ambushed a group of marchers. One officer attacked a woman and her ailing father. When her son, 26-year-old Jimmy Lee Jackson, stepped in, the trooper shot him at close range. Jackson died two days later.

Jackson's funeral drew 200 mourners and an angry sermon from Martin Luther King, Jr. Who killed Jimmy Lee Jackson? He was killed, King declared, by every lawless sheriff, every racist politician from governors on down, every passive white minister, every black who "stands on the sidelines in the struggle for justice." But no speech by King lacked a note of hope.

Martin Luther King, Jr., delivers a funeral oration for 26-year-old Jimmy Lee Jackson of Marion, Alabama. Jackson had been shot by a state trooper for trying to rescue his mother and grandfather from an attack by troopers during a 1965 civil rights march.

He ended by urging blacks to strive with all their might "to make the American dream a reality."

To arouse public opinion over the mistreatment of blacks seeking the ballot, King planned a march from Selma to Montgomery to petition Governor George Wallace for protection of voting rights. Six hundred blacks gathered outside Brown Chapel African Methodist Episcopal Church on Sunday morning, March 7, 1965, to begin the 54-mile trek. At the head of the line were SNCC's John Lewis and the Reverend Hosea Williams, an aide to King. They walked toward the Edmund Pettus Bridge. There, they found Jim Clark's posse and a host of state troopers armed and waiting.

"John, can you swim?" whispered Williams to Lewis. "No," said Lewis. "I can't either," confided Williams, "and I'm sure we're gonna end up in that river." Ordered by the state troopers to forget their march, the blacks bowed their heads in a prayerful manner but did not retreat. Suddenly the troopers rushed forward in a flying wedge, clubs ready to strike. Almost alone among the marchers, John Lewis held his ground. He fell from the first blow by the troopers. Further blows sent other blacks to the ground screaming and clutching their heads; white onlookers cheered. Then, as blacks ran or limped in all directions, Sheriff Clark turned loose his mounted posse. They charged with a yell, swinging bullwhips at the fleeing marchers.

That night, the nation's television networks stunned viewers with scenes of white police on a rampage against peaceful, unarmed blacks. People across the country responded in shock, anger, and near disbelief that racism remained so strong, so savage. Many Americans telephoned and sent telegrams and letters to their congressmen, asking them, in the words of an editor from Chippewa, Wisconsin, to stop "this bloody disregard of Americans' constitutional rights." The editor added that "we and the many citizens who have contacted us" generally did not like federal interference in local affairs. But, he said, "It is not a time for words; it is a time for action."

From the White House, Lyndon Johnson monitored the events in Selma with growing fury. He had already planned to ask for a voting rights act, but he now felt that "Bloody Sunday," as blacks spoke of the March 7 brutality, called for more than sending a routine request to Congress. On Monday evening, March 15, Johnson personally entered the House of Representatives to make his case for a powerful new civil rights law.

The president began slowly, amid a hush so complete that even the clicks of photographers' cameras sounded clearly in the chamber. Johnson warned the legislators and the public that if America defeated

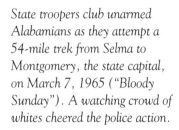

State troopers club unarmed Alabamians as they attempt a 54-mile trek from Selma to Montgomery, the state capital, on March 7, 1965 ("Bloody Sunday"). A watching crowd of whites cheered the police action.

every enemy, doubled its wealth, conquered the stars, and yet failed to resolve this issue, "then we will have failed as a people and as a nation."

Continuing at a faster pace, Johnson said Selma marked a turning point in American history. What happened there was "part of a far larger movement . . . the effort of American Negroes to secure for themselves the full blessings of American life." Then, thumbs raised, fists clenched, radiating determination, Johnson declared, "Their cause must be our cause, too. Because it is not just Negroes, but really all of us who must overcome . . . bigotry and injustice." He concluded with a pledge that brought tears to the eyes of Martin Luther King, Jr.: And "we shall . . . overcome."

On Sunday, March 21, 1965, a crowd gathered at Brown Chapel to begin again the journey to Montgomery. This time there were some important changes in the scene. Thanks to Johnson's commitment to protect the marchers, state troopers stayed back while federal marshals and Alabama National Guardsmen flanked the roadside, and helicopters scouted for signs of danger. The assembly at the chapel had also grown from the original band of 500 to several thousand, including many from outside Selma.

Standing in front of the chapel, King offered a special welcome to poor blacks who might have felt out of place among the many middle-class, educated marchers: "Those of us who are Negroes don't have much. We have known the long night of poverty. Because of the system, we don't have much education and some of us don't know how to make our nouns and verbs agree. But thank God we have our bodies, our feet, and our souls." King's aide Ralph Abernathy urged the crowd on with the promise, "Wallace, it's all over now." Following these brief speeches, Highway 80 filled with people stepping toward Montgomery, eager to bring Wallace the news.

A glance at the masses trudging along the roadside reflected the wide range of groups in the country now united in support of black civil rights. Black ministers directed the march, but white clergymen were prominent as well. Among them strode Rabbi Abraham Joshua Heschel, whose tall figure, massive beard, and flowing hair led one marcher to exclaim, "Why, there is the Lord!"

Assistant Attorney General John Doar marched, too, to see that everyone enjoyed full safety, as President Johnson had directed. White marchers who had flown to Alabama from as far as California found a model of determination in one-legged James Letherer of Michigan, who pressed forward on crutches, regretting his real handicap—that he couldn't "do more to help these people." Seventeen-year-old Joe Boone, arrested seven times in the Selma campaign, explained that his mother and father never thought this day would come. "But it's here," he said, "and I want to do my part." So, too, did Cager Lee, Jimmy Lee Jackson's 78-year-old grandfather, who could march only a few miles a day but always returned the next, saying, "Just got to tramp some more."

At the head of the massive, joyous assembly was the Reverend Martin Luther King, Jr., strolling in shirtsleeves, chatting now with his wife, now with John Lewis or some other aide, joking easily with reporters, clearly relishing the event. Although he did not walk the entire 54 miles, having left on Tuesday amid new rumors of an assassination plot, his presence dominated the march. As the black journal *Ebony* noted, cameramen and reporters strained to catch "every twist of the mouth and wrinkle of the forehead of leader King." To many blacks who joined the march or lined its path to Montgomery, he appeared set apart by God for a mission of deliverance.

The road to Montgomery led the marchers across flat farmlands, rough cotton patches, freshly plowed red fields, and pine thickets. The pilgrims' lively singing kept up even when the lanes veered into dim swamps, where ghostly Spanish moss covered the still waters and dead tree stumps. Rain drenched the marchers on the third day but failed to dampen their spirits. A black man boomed out a chant like an old slave spiritual—"Lift 'em up and lay 'em down, we are coming from Selma town!"—and people pushed forward to the beat. Along the roadside, spectators answered the call-and-response greetings from one or another of the marchers:

What do you want?
Freedom
When do you want it?
Now!
Where are we going?
Montgomery!

On Thursday, the fifth day of the march, the ever-growing crowd sang spirituals under raised umbrellas, then followed King through a misty drizzle into Montgomery. March 25, 1965, was a day for testimony, by famous speakers and by ordinary black townsfolk who had tried to register but could not. As

the sun slowly disappeared behind the capitol, King at last addressed the crowd.

"We are on the move now," he told his listeners, and no wave of racism, no burning of churches, no bombing of homes, no clubbing and killing of clergymen and young people would stop the march for freedom. Yes, King said, "There are still some difficult days ahead. We are still in for a season of suffering." But he assured them, in a pledge of faith in both God and man: "It will not be long, because truth pressed to earth will rise again."

> How long?
> Not long, because no lie can live forever.
> How long?
> Not long, because you will reap what you sow.
> How long?
> Not long, because the arc of the moral universe is long but it bends toward justice.

Martin Luther King, Jr. (center, in front of flag), and his wife, Coretta, lead marchers on the last stretch of the Selma-to-Montgomery walk on March 25, 1965. Other participants include (front row, left to right) A. Philip Randolph, John Lewis, and the Reverend Ralph Abernathy. Marching fifth from the left is Nobel Prize winner Ralph Bunche, and holding a child at right is the Reverend Hosea Williams.

Watched by his sons, Thurgood junior (left) and John William; his wife, Cissy; and President Lyndon Johnson, Thurgood Marshall is sworn in as the first African American U.S. solicitor general. Afterward, Johnson said it would be good for "schoolchildren to know that when the great United States government spoke in the highest court in the land, it did so through a Negro."

King swept on to a thundering conclusion:

Glory, glory, hallelujah!
Glory, glory hallelujah!
Glory, glory hallelujah!

The audience, now swollen to 25,000, sang the movement's anthem—altered to express the sense of triumph by the march and all it represented: "We Have Overcome Today."

Four months later, Lyndon Johnson, white Texan and sometime opponent of civil rights legislation, once more proved his commitment to black equality: to the post of U.S. solicitor general (the nation's third highest legal position, after attorney general and assistant attorney general), he nominated Thurgood Marshall, one of America's most effective lawyers and a legendary figure of the civil rights movement.

In his new job, Marshall, the first black citizen to hold it, became the nation's top-ranking courtroom advocate. Asked why he accepted the job—which, while prestigious, paid less than he received as a federal judge—Marshall said, "I believe that in this time, especially, we do what our government requests of us. Negroes have made great advances in government and I think it's time they started making some sacrifices."

One month after he appointed Marshall solicitor general, on August 6, Johnson signed the landmark Voting Rights Act of 1965. Earlier civil rights laws had allowed federal officials to prosecute racist registrars in court, but the process was often agonizingly slow. The new law empowered government officials, whenever they found signs of discrimination, to take immediate charge of local registration and election centers. The act also outlawed tests for knowledge, character, and "literacy" as requirements for voter registration. Millions of southern blacks now added their names to the voting rolls, resulting in the sudden respectful dependence of white politicians on black voters.

8

EPILOGUE:
NEW CHALLENGES

THE civil rights movement wrought a revolution in American race relations. "White" and "colored" signs suddenly came down from the hotels, rest rooms, theaters, and other public places where they had hung for generations. Integration moved more slowly in education, but in time, most southern public schools started putting black and white children in the same classrooms. The federal government also cracked down on hate groups like the Ku Klux Klan. The Klan lost much of its influence beginning in 1964, when FBI agents slipped into its ranks and sent detailed reports of its crimes and membership back to headquarters.

Civil rights campaigns won their greatest success in restoring southern blacks' right to the ballot. Until 1964, only about 40 percent of the South's black adults were registered to vote, a figure that shrank to about 5 percent in Mississippi, where racial violence kept blacks in constant terror. In 1964, barely 100 blacks held political office in the entire country. The Voting Rights Act of 1965 changed all that:

Urban children play near a refuse-filled vacant lot. Even after the enormous achievements of the civil rights movement, large segments of the nation's black population faced ongoing poverty and discrimination in housing and employment.

within 25 years, southern black voter registration rose to nearly two-thirds, and well over 7,000 blacks, among them some 300 mayors, occupied American political offices.

A clear majority of these officials served in the South. In Alabama's Black Belt, where Bull Connor and Jim Clark once met civil rights marchers with attack dogs and cattle prods, nearly every county elected a black sheriff. Mississippi changed most dramatically, registering about three-quarters of its voting-age blacks and electing more than 600 black officials, the nation's highest total.

The civil rights movement ended a tradition of racist laws that had held down African Americans for centuries. As important as these changes were, however, they could not destroy racism all at once. Civil rights leaders soon found the remaining problems at least as challenging—and urgent—as those they had overcome.

In the northern ghettos, reformers soon learned, racism could work its harm even without the open support of Jim Crow laws. Real estate agents and white homeowners privately arranged not to sell or lease to blacks who tried to escape overcrowded slum neighborhoods. Poverty, too, trapped the mass of blacks in the ghetto. In 1960, nearly half of all black families lived below the federal poverty line of $3,000 for a family of four. Black family income was little more than half that of white families, and the rate of unemployment for black adults (over 10 percent) and teenagers (almost 25 percent) was about twice the rate for whites.

The history of America—"land of opportunity"—had been shaped by immigrant groups who worked their way from poverty to middle-class comfort. Blacks, however, found their hopes blocked by color lines at every point. Because many industries openly refused to employ them, they were forced to accept

"Negro" jobs—servants' or unskilled workers' positions with low pay, little security, and less chance for promotions or raises. Some unions welcomed blacks, but others, especially those in the construction industry, did not.

The effects of lasting poverty due to racial barriers bred other ills among blacks. Of some 60,000 drug addicts known to the U.S. Bureau of Narcotics at the end of 1966, just over half were blacks. Juvenile delinquency, dependence on welfare, school truancy, dropouts, and illiteracy occurred far more frequently in black ghettos than in surrounding areas. Crime of every kind plagued the black slums, and among young adult black males, the main cause of death was homicide.

The crippling features of black slum life wounded or destroyed youthful hopes. With fathers often absent and mothers at work, many children looked to gang leaders, hustlers, dope peddlers, and numbers runners as models for survival. Before reaching young manhood, boys took on the bitter attitudes of older males; in a nation where a man's worth was measured in dollars, they felt cut off from opportunity.

These harsh conditions, often magnified by tensions with white police, produced frequent acts of violence. Complaints about police abuses—racist remarks, arrests on doubtful grounds, beatings of unresisting residents—were part of daily conversation in the ghettos. The task of police officers was not merely thankless but largely hopeless; even the smallest spark could set off a chain reaction of rage. That is what happened in the Los Angeles ghetto called Watts on a week that began in 98-degree heat and ended in a smoldering wasteland.

In the early evening of August 11, 1965, California highway patrolman Lee Minikus pulled over 21-year-old Marquette Frye for weaving dangerously in traffic. Already gathered in the street, seeking relief from the fourth sizzling day of a heat wave, residents gravitated toward the scene. By all accounts, Minikus was courteous, smiling at Frye's jokes and bantering with bystanders. Nevertheless, he found the youth clearly drunk and unable even to produce his license. Frye's mother, Rena, at first took the officer's side, scolding her son for driving drunk and urging him to go quietly and make it easy on himself. But in the ghetto, where a policeman was viewed as "The Man"—as a hostile intruder rather than a peace officer—the mood of bystanders could change suddenly.

Marquette Frye panicked at the thought of jail and pulled angrily away from Minikus. Backup police and local residents poured onto the street, the tension growing amid muttered curses of the "blue-eyed" cops. As Frye suddenly lunged for Minikus's nightstick, his older brother Ronald Frye, fearing a general police attack, rushed over to an officer nearby. Meanwhile, newly arrived patrolman John Wilson decided his fellow officers needed rescue from 150 angry blacks. He charged straight on. One blow of Wilson's nightstick doubled over Ronald Frye, and two more sent Marquette to the ground.

No longer in sympathy with the policemen, Rena Frye leapt onto Minikus's back, but police officers soon pried her loose and herded her, along with her sons, into a police squad car. An onlooker screamed, "We've got no rights at all—it's just like Selma!" Another shouted, "Come on, let's get them."

Had this been a comfortable middle-class suburb, the anger might have been quieted by a desire to maintain order and property values. But this was Watts, a dense, dirty ghetto where too many—more than 250,000—residents were crammed into too few faded buildings (statistically, 27.3 people lived on each acre of Watts; in Los Angeles County as a whole, the figure was 7.4 people per acre). Trash collection was a rare event in Watts, so a stroll along any street

Theddis Roosevelt Coney, 38, son of Louisiana sharecroppers, takes a call in his office—that of U.S. marshal for the Southern District of Texas. By 1977, a black southern sheriff, a concept almost unthinkable a decade earlier, had become routine.

meant walking amid broken glass, rusty cans, and rotting food. Two-thirds of the residents were on welfare, and over one-third of the adult males were jobless. Watts's population was 98 percent black; 200 of the district's 205 officers were white. Nothing about Watts made it likely that people would "keep cool" after the arrest of Marquette Frye. And nobody did keep cool.

Fourteen thousand National Guardsmen and several thousand local police needed six days to stop the arson, rock throwing, looting, and sniping that now swept Watts. The violence left 34 people dead. Nine hundred people suffered injuries, and four thousand were arrested for violence, vandalism, looting, loiter-

ing, or simply walking by a policeman at the wrong time. Hundreds of families were left homeless, and shopkeepers found their stores charred and plundered. The damage came to some $45 million. Amid the wreckage, civil rights leaders such as Roy Wilkins left

In another sign of changing times, a black Miamian tells a hooded orator where to go. Said the African American to the Ku Klux Klansman: "Take your racial problem elsewhere."

behind their hopes of ending what Wilkins called "all the years of oppression," realizing that instead, they "were just beginning a new ordeal."

Martin Luther King, Jr., saw firsthand the desperation behind this violence as he toured the ruins of

Watts. When a group of youngsters declared joyously, "We won!" King asked, "How can you say you won when 34 Negroes are dead, your community is destroyed, and whites are using the riots as an excuse for inaction [on black rights]?" "We won," the youths insisted, "because we made them pay attention to us."

King confessed that the destruction said something about the limits of the civil rights movement. It seemed more than a coincidence that Watts exploded just five days after President Johnson had proudly signed the Voting Rights Bill into law. Residents of Watts, Harlem, or Chicago's West Side slums could read about southern black victories in their local papers. Yet their own lives remained as bleak as before the Greensboro sit-in.

Ghetto dwellers, who lived in poverty and segregation despite having the ballot and other civil rights, felt drawn to movements that preached black pride, black unity, and black independence from the wider society. The most powerful of these groups was the Nation of Islam, popularly known as the Black Muslims. Under its leader, Elijah Muhammad, this group swept across the ghettos in the 1960s, proclaiming black superiority and rejecting all things white.

The Nation of Islam did much to reform ex-convicts, improve family life, and open shops that raised living conditions in the ghetto. But to whites the Black Muslims came to symbolize racial hatred, to stand as a threat to white America and to the civil rights leaders who asked only for racial integration and equal opportunity. The main target of white fears was the Nation's chief recruiter, a brilliant and fearless speaker known as Malcolm X.

Born Malcolm Little in Omaha, Nebraska, in 1925, Malcolm X was a striking example of black rebirth from self-hatred and misery in the slums. A school dropout, drug user, and petty criminal, he went to jail at the age of 21 for attempted burglary. In prison

Attending a 1964 Nation of Islam convention in Chicago, a Black Muslim sells newspapers picturing the movement's founder, Elijah Muhammad. In the 1960s, the Nation of Islam gained immense popularity by proclaiming black superiority and scorning white society.

he met a follower of Elijah Muhammad, who led him suddenly to see white people as his enemy and prison as the most recent stage in a lifetime of locked doors. Muhammad called for establishment of an all-black state, a call that became a rallying cry for black nationalists.

After he was freed from prison in 1952, Malcolm X became a sharp-tongued critic of the civil rights movement, and he began to recruit thousands of followers for the Nation of Islam. When he spoke to urban slum dwellers, Malcolm cut to their deep nerve

Black Muslim minister Malcolm X meets with Egyptian educators during a 1964 visit to the Middle East. Although he originally called for an all-black state and sneered at Martin Luther King, Jr., and his belief in nonviolence, Malcolm later reached out to King and endorsed "a society in which people can live like human beings on a basis of equality."

of pain and anger. "You cannot find one black man," he said, "I do not care who he is, who has not been personally damaged in some way by the devilish acts [of white people]."

Unlike King, Malcolm offered no hope that whites or American society could change for the better. Instead he called on blacks to unite and take control, "by any means necessary," of their own land, work, and culture. Blacks, he insisted, should not seek "to integrate into this corrupt society, but to separate from it, to a land of our own, where we can reform ourselves, lift up our moral standards, and try to be godly."

Malcolm X scorned the civil rights movement's belief in nonviolence. Blacks, he said, needed a revolution, and "revolution is bloody." King spoke of his dream, but Malcolm warned, "the black masses in America were—and still are—having a nightmare." In 1959, the Nation of Islam claimed 12,000 members; one year later, the number had risen to 100,000.

Poor blacks in the ghetto admired Malcolm X for his courage and loved him for giving them pride in being black. Yet he longed to do more, and he felt privately troubled that while civil rights workers were risking their lives for freedom, the Black Muslims were doing little to change American society or politics. Late in 1963, already out of favor with Elijah Muhammad, Malcolm drifted away from the Nation of Islam to find a new approach to change.

Traveling in Africa and the Middle East, Malcolm found whites who showed no prejudice but who instead shared his commitment to racial justice. He decided then that whites were not naturally evil, but rather were led to do evil by "America's racist society." To change that system, Malcolm now looked not to one race but to a new generation: "The young whites, and blacks, too, are the only hope that America has."

Malcolm began reaching out to civil rights leaders, talking about the importance of the ballot as a possible alternative to violent revolution. He even attended the NAACP's annual meeting in 1964. At about that time, a Canadian interviewer asked if he still believed in a black state. Malcolm answered, "No, I believe in a society in which people can live like human beings on a basis of equality."

Early in February 1965 Malcolm traveled to Selma, Alabama, where Martin Luther King, Jr., had been jailed for leading the voting-rights campaign. Although King's aides feared that Malcolm would stir up hate among the blacks, Malcolm said only that whites should listen to King; if they did not, he warned,

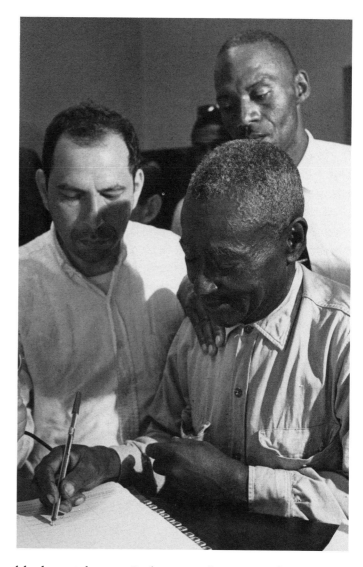

Tom Flowers signs the voting roll at Panola County Courthouse in Batesville, Mississippi, in 1966. Prepared to vote for the first time in his 68 years, Flowers said he had been inspired by hearing Robert Moses speak at a Mississippi Freedom March rally.

blacks might try "other ways" to win their rights. Afterward Malcolm told King's wife, Coretta: "I didn't come to Selma to make his job difficult. I really did come thinking I could make it easier. If the white people realize what the alternative is, perhaps they will be more willing to hear Dr. King."

Eighteen days later, Malcolm X was murdered in Harlem by three Black Muslims. He was still seeking a path that could lead blacks and whites, peacefully if possible, toward a just society. So, too, were King and other civil rights leaders, as they groped for answers to the racial divisions and hatred in the country.

The explosion of human pain and frustration in the ghettos showed that the ills of racism could not be cured by civil rights laws alone. It would take a hard struggle to change racial attitudes and overcome the forces that still trapped millions of blacks in squalor and segregation. King and other civil rights reformers remained hopeful about the possibilities for peaceful democratic change, no matter how difficult the challenge. That faith had taken the movement a long way across a difficult path, toppling Jim Crow barriers that had long seemed rock-solid. Now, as they resumed their journey toward racial equality, civil rights leaders held fast to their belief that the dream of equal justice would continue to inspire the nation.

FURTHER READING

Holt, Len. *The Summer That Didn't End*. London: William Heinemann, 1965.

King, Martin Luther, Jr. *Why We Can't Wait*. New York: New American Library, 1964.

Malcolm X with Alex Haley. *The Autobiography of Malcolm X*. New York: Ballantine, 1965.

Oates, Stephen J. *Let the Trumpet Sound: The Life of Martin Luther King, Jr*. New York: Harper and Row, 1982.

Raines, Howell, ed. *My Soul Is Rested: Movement Days in the Deep South Remembered*. New York: Penguin, 1983.

Sellers, Cleveland, with Robert Terrell. *The River of No Return: The Autobiography of a Black Militant and the Life and Death of SNCC*. New York: William Morrow, 1973.

Williams, Juan, with the "Eyes on the Prize" production team. *Eyes on the Prize: America's Civil Rights Years, 1954–1965*. New York: Viking, 1987.

Wolff, Miles, Jr. *Lunch at the Five & Ten*. New York: Stein and Day, 1970.

Zinn, Howard. *SNCC: The New Abolitionists*. 2nd ed. Boston: Beacon Press, 1965.

INDEX

PICTURE CREDITS

ROBERT WEISBROT, a native of New York City, is the Christian A. Johnson Distinguished Teaching Professor of History at Colby College in Maine. He is the author of *Father Divine* in Chelsea House's BLACK AMERICANS OF ACHIEVEMENT series. His most recent book is the highly acclaimed *Freedom Bound: A History of America's Civil Rights Movement* (Penguin, 1991).

CLAYBORNE CARSON, senior consulting editor of the MILESTONES IN BLACK AMERICAN HISTORY series, is a professor of history at Stanford University. His first book, *In Struggle: SNCC and the Black Awakening of the 1960s* (1981), won the Frederick Jackson Turner Prize of the Organization of American Historians. He is the director of the Martin Luther King, Jr., Papers Project, which will publish 12 volumes of King's writings.

DARLENE CLARK HINE, senior consulting editor of the MILESTONES IN BLACK AMERICAN HISTORY series, is the John A. Hannah Professor of American History at Michigan State University. She is the author of numerous books and articles on black women's history. Her most recent work is the two-volume *Black Women in America: An Historical Encyclopedia* (1993).